As We Were

An Essex family during and after the Second World War

Nan Collecott

With love & best wishes to Katrina & Dominic

Nan Collecott   *1993*

Blue Button Press

As We Were

An Essex family during and after the Second World War

Nan Collecott is the author of
Peggles and Primroses, a Country Childhood in the Twenties and Thirties
pub: Terence Dalton, Lavenham, Suffolk, 1989

Blue Button Press is an imprint of Alpha Word Power
3 Bluecoat Buildings, Claypath, Durham DH1 1RF
tel: 091-384-7219; fax: 091-384-3767

Contents

Illustrations

Foreword

Here is a piece of social history, meticulously observed and presented in an engaging style.

In her first book, *Peggles and Primroses*, Nan Collecott drew an enchanting picture of her childhood in the Essex countryside.

As We Were carries on the story, beginning with the outbreak of war in September 1939, which incidentally coincided with her return from her honeymoon, until the 1970s. It portrays the shocks of war, the severe privations which followed, and the changes in outlook in national and family life.

This well-documented account of how we lived then, during those thirty years, will stir memories for older readers, and will intrigue those who have grown up since those times.

It is the product of a lively mind and makes absorbing reading.

Dora Saint ('Miss Read')

Acknowledgements

I should like to thank all those friends, acquaintances and strangers who wrote to me after reading my first book, *Peggles and Primroses*, and for the encouragement it gave me to write this book.

I am also grateful to all the following: Lady Gladys Atkins, Helen Clapp, Jean Martin, Amy and Roger Pring, Norah Read, Dick Rowe, Betty and Francis Smith, and Judy Tinney. In particular, I owe a great debt to Claire and Mike Meixner for taking photographs, providing information and for all their enthusiastic encouragement.

I am most grateful to the American 834th Engineer Aviation Group for allowing me access to their privately published commemorative book, *Thus We Served*, and to use information and pictures. My thanks also to Bob Mynn and Dick Rowe for their help in gaining this information.

I thank Peter Hughes of Blue Button Press for his enthusiasm and understanding in producing this book, and Lotte Shankland for her help with aspects of its design.

My appreciation also goes to Dora Saint (better known as "Miss Read", author of *Thrushcross Green* and many other much-loved books), for so kindly writing a foreword.

I must also thank my family, who, albeit reluctantly, allowed me to use photographs from their childhood. My special thanks go to Diana who has given much more time than she can spare to reading and editing the manuscript, and to offering me invaluable advice.

Nan Collecott, June 1993

1:     The author, 1937

2:     G, 1939

For G
with love and gratitude

Chapter I

1939, War and Marriage

A thump on the front door. An impatient voice shouted, "Put that light out!" World War Two had begun that morning. G and I were totally unprepared.

We had returned from our honeymoon just two weeks before to the Victorian semi we had lovingly decorated and furnished, overlooking the pond and Green at Buckhurst Hill, in Essex. Black-out material had not been one of our purchases; in fact we had obliterated the impending threat of war, the ridiculous pictures of strutting Nazis and the perversion of children in the Hitler Youth, from our mind in an all-pervading romantic haze. We were rudely awakened.

G, ever practical, dug out some thin grey blankets bequeathed to us by his mother and we safety-pinned them across the living-room curtains, struggling to prevent strips of light escaping at the edges. I had grown up in an Essex village and was no stranger to candles and paraffin lamps, stumbling along dark passages and lanes, or groping in cupboards. Remembering to switch off the light in the hall before opening the front door was not so easy. Outdoors all the street lights had gone out.

We had no idea what war would mean to us: I was born in 1913 so remembered very little of World War 1, except the hard life my energetic little mother led while my father, almost a stranger, was absent at the front for four years. G was four years older than I and had lived in Leytonstone in East London, so he had clearer memories; but he shared my eternal optimism. We were happy and in love; we faced the unknown with some apprehension, but with an alert anticipation and a naïve confidence.

There was so little time to settle in, to enjoy our first home together; so little time to talk. The phoney war started immediately. G and I had met when we were both teaching at the Wellington Avenue Schools in Chingford, he in the Boys' school and I in the Girls'. The days of co-education were a long way off.

We had been summoned to a staff meeting that morning, September 3rd, and had stood round a small radio listening to Neville Chamberlain's ominous announcement that Britain was at war. No-one spoke; my headmistress was in tears. I don't know if the others were filled with noble patriotic thoughts; I, who longed to be a pacifist, but felt Nazism was an evil with which I could not compromise, was conscious of the futility of war and of the possibility that G would be called up while I would face the loneliness my mother had felt. I think we all comforted ourselves with the thought that the war would soon be over; six years was unthinkable at that time.

3: Our first house (on the left) at 6 Hills Road, Buckhurst Hill

4: Buckhurst Hill: the Green

Chapter I

While we were attempting to behave as if nothing had altered, and making plans for the coming term, the banshee wailing of the siren reminded us that nothing was normal. Fortunately the Air Raid warning was a false alarm and someone had mistaken a friendly aircraft for an enemy plane; the long drawn-out siren announced the All Clear. They were sounds to become all too familiar. Throughout the Blitz, in the daytime and every night, that heart-stopping undulating wail interrupted every activity, demanding action: I still hate the sound of factory sirens.

Hand-in-hand we strolled back to Buckhurst Hill across the plain and through the woods, swinging our little brown boxes containing the compulsory issue of gas masks which would accompany us everywhere. We tried them on at home and stared at each other's grotesque faces. They were a frightening barrier between us, but we wrenched them off and laughed; to contemplate wearing them for real was too awful.

It was ironical that I had been summoned to that staff meeting. At the end of the summer term we had married and I had resigned my job. This was not my desire, because we desperately needed the money and I enjoyed teaching; but it was compulsory. Married women teachers were not allowed. Men were the great providers; their wives must remain at home, bring up the children and not occupy posts which men or unmarried women could fill. I had reluctantly said goodbye to all the girls at the school, persuaded them that there was no way that I could stay on. Then I had left laden with dozens of present bought with their precious pocket money, and promises to come back and see them. I left too with a promise to myself, which has taken me fifty years to fulfil, that I would now find time to write that book I had so often begun with a spurt of enthusiasm and abandoned with equal despair.

As soon as war was declared I was requested to report back to the same school. Tremendous plans had already been made for evacuation to the country and I was needed. With gratitude we learned that the two schools were to go to the same area and that G and I could stay together. We all had some misgivings that the area chosen was around Rochford in Essex; the proximity to Southend airport seemed disastrous. We failed to see that it was any safer than our outer suburb of London on the edge of Epping Forest, which was in London's Green Belt. But no-one asked our opinion; we were all part of some master plan.

We were issued with a suggested list of items to buy and take with us. I can only remember Keatings Powder because I was not convinced that it was necessary. I soon found out how wrong I was. We had to splash it around everywhere and even then the odd flea floated on the water when we had baths.

5:      With G and my mother at Wellington Avenue School, Chingford

Most of the reports I have read since of the evacuation, stress the misery of children separated from parents for the first time, the floods of tears, the sad partings. We were lucky. I have no recollection of any distressing scenes, perhaps because ours were senior schools and all the children were over eleven, or perhaps because they were new schools and, other than the two Heads, all members of staff were young. We were one of three couples married that summer and there were other romantic attachments. I think the children thought it would be quite like a holiday. Most of them were familiar with Southend, and their parents would have no difficulty in visiting them by train or bus. It was not yet the age of the car, but public transport was so far quite efficient.

The schools had five or six hundred pupils and a convoy of London double-decker buses transported us to the town of Rochford, where billeting officers with lists of addresses and numbers were waiting, surrounded by women who had either offered to take in evacuees or had had their spare room commandeered. We tried to keep families and friends together as far as possible, but arrangements were swept out of our hands. We were teachers and not expected to interfere with the billeting officers' conscientious plans. They had visited every house, mansion, and cottage for miles around, noted the number of rooms which could be available, and refused to let anyone, rich or poor, avoid opening their doors unless there was a very good reason. It should be said, too, that very few people tried to dodge evacuees however disrupting they might prove; we were met by warm and kindly people, genuinely wanting to help and to make the children feel at home. They looked the children over as they dismounted, and a particularly determined, and maybe discerning, woman pushed forward, seized two children, and proceeded off home with them. It was easy to place the tidily-dressed, the smiling and those who needed mothering; not so easy for volunteer parents to choose from those who were stubbornly uncommunicative or had a wicked gleam in their eye. They were accepted with good grace, but some reluctance.

It took a long time to sort everyone out, but they all had temporary homes for the night and we would visit them in the morning to sort out any real misfits.

Billets had been organised for the staff too. G and I were whisked off to a small neat terraced house in Rochford where we were welcomed by a kind middle-aged widow, slim, quiet and rather staid. She showed us into her front room, which was to be our living room and left us to prepare supper.

We looked around us in horror. It was not a room to live in. It was a show case. Everything was spotless, but every surface was smothered with small bric-à-brac. I might be able to prevent G swiping a vase off the mantlepiece, but if he turned round suddenly some of the dozens of little china souvenirs on the round table in the middle of the room would certainly be in danger. And who was going to keep such a room dusted? It appalled me. I couldn't see how we could eat, work or relax there.

We accepted the arrangement for a few days until we knew our hostess better and then I plucked up courage and suggested to her that we should live with her and leave her treasures intact. She agreed at once; I think she was lonely and grateful for the company. She soon sorted me out. My haphazarded method of hanging out the washing bothered her; she was soon demonstrating exactly how I should pin up G's shirts on the line; and she never was satisfied that I took enough care with the ironing.

October 1939 was a warm and glowing Indian summer. There were no more false alarms and we were lulled into a belief that war would not affect us much. It was unsettling and unnatural. We could only teach for half a day because we had to share the premises of the Rochford Senior School and there was no room for us all together. Stupid things began to niggle; the blackboard had been cleaned when work on it was needed. Miss Stewart, our Headmistress, a charming and cultured woman, but nevertheless a feminist, found the men's staff irritating and chauvinistic; they found her withdrawn and disturbing, and suspected her of feeling superior. The Headmaster was completely out of his depth with her. She suffered for all the injustices in the world and her face showed a strange haunted look like Virginia Woolf's; he felt a little common-sense was all that was required. She asked me once in a hurt and shocked voice, "Do you really agree that the wheels creak when women undertake anything?" He had evidently been goaded beyond endurance by her perfectionist attitude. I loved and respected her; she had a great influence on me as a young teacher joining her team straight from college. I hated to see her unhappy and unable to adapt to sharing with the men. She longed to get back to Chingford.

The children were soon restless too. Their parents were living normal lives back home and there seemed no reason for them to stay. Those who were homesick, and those who thought it would be a good way to dispense with education, dribbled back. Some found the country a new and absorbing life, particularly if they were billeted on a farm with animals; others in remote cottages with privies in the garden were amazed and affronted. There were bound to be misfits and if they were in the villages it was not easy for staff to visit often. Only the headmaster and one member of staff had a car. However, the weather was balmy and it was good to walk, if time–consuming. We had to move a few to more congenial billets. Some had a long walk to school, which was no particular hardship in good weather, but even so, some protested. They were not used to it and often had no suitable shoes. The quiet and the loneliness upset some: they missed the busyness of Chingford streets, the close–knit communities, the shops around the corner. No transport, no fish and chips and no 'flicks' – it was an unfamiliar world.

Whenever we could find free evenings, G and I caught the bus into Southend and walked the length of the sea front from the shell–fish booths in Leigh, past Westcliff poised on the hill and the jumble of activity by Southend pier as far as the end of the esplanade at Thorpe Bay. It was good to feel a sea breeze and smell the mud, and to enjoy it without hundreds of bodies jostling for space on the beach or screams of youngsters terrifying themselves on the enormous helter–skelter in the Kursaal. It was playing at being on holiday: we were restless too.

Without warning an official letter arrived – short and to the point. Essex Education Committee thanked me for my help in an emergency but no longer needed my services which would be terminated at the end of the month.

However, ever confident and optimistic, we recovered our sense of proportion and went into one of our frequent huddles on High Finance. G was meticulous with figures as he taught Maths and metalwork; I had never progressed beyond School Certificate Maths and was fundamentally uninterested in it, but if he kept it simple, I could follow his basic arguments. We brooded over a sheet of figures. But no amount of rearrangement under the present circumstances would provide a possible solution. It was patently obvious that threes into G's salary would not go.

'Threes' needs some explanation. We had not broadcast our peculiar situation, and under normal circumstances were quite sanguine about it. However, we now had to make rapid readjustments.

6: Bancroft's, where G went to school

Ten years earlier, G's mother had found married life intolerable and walked out on her husband, expecting her two sons to set up a home and provide for her. They did so, accepting, too readily as we later agreed, that she was the wronged party. It was a bizarre situation. The boys were nineteen and twenty-one, kind and idealistic, when they made such an undertaking, and for ten years they had supported her entirely. She had no income, was too young for a pension at first, would not hear of making the separation legal and had no motivation to find a job. She was absorbed with her "difficult situation" and constantly reminded them of it and, bowled over by her helplessness, they felt a loyalty to her which inevitably became a burden. Neither of them really loved her, but in the climate of the time they did their duty, and until they married no great problems arose.

G had come into teaching late, having worked in the London offices of Sage's, the shop-window fitters, on leaving Bancroft's School at Woodford Green. It was a job with good prospects, but he felt a need to be more closely involved with people, and particularly young people. He had worked with Bancroft's Mission in the East End in his spare time, and now decided to take up teaching. This meant seeing himself through college, which he did by working all hours of the day and night at ASEA, the Anglo-Swedish electrical company in Walthamstow.

While G was in college he was unable to share with his older brother, Rob, who was a qualified electrical engineer, in supporting his mother. In order to repay Rob, G had to take on full responsibility for a few years after he left college. And this is where I came in.

In spite of the financial problems we decided to get married. Rob was already married to a very talented graduate of the Royal School of Needlework; they were expecting their first baby and had bought their own home. G's mother was devastated that G too was going to marry. What would happen to her? We managed to set her up in a small flat in Woodford and sell the house they had lived in together. We doubted her ability to make a life for herself, but it seemed a reasonable solution.

Yet, juggle with figures as we might, there was no way that I could stay with G in Rochford without a salary, or go back to our new abandoned home and run a separate life, while still supporting his mother. Threes into one would not go.

A phone call to my parents settled it for the time being. "Your room's still here," they cheerfully said, "Come on home for a bit."

They were always warm and generous; I gratefully accepted their offer.

Chapter II

Evacuees in Matching

I returned to Matching Tye, my home village, with mixed feelings. I had made the break and left with high hopes. I felt I was putting the clock back, but this was mistaken. It looked the same sleepy village, but was now, in fact, a Reception Area, and my father was the billeting officer. There were new faces in the cottages: mothers and children from the East End of London. Not all of them were going to enjoy staying in such a remote and still primitive village; not all the inhabitants would welcome criticism from visitors who probably enjoyed more civilised amenities in their homes. Cockneys proverbially thought us dim; and we thought them vulgar. The next few months were to dispel many of the myths and prejudices.

Woodville, our house pressed up against Matching Wood for shelter, was not the same either. Wide white gates, dividing tall clipped hedges, gave no hint of change. Flower beds were a little dejected, but late roses still flourished; even our Dorothy Perkin and American Pillar rambling roses made a brave show, scattering dry browning petals over the grass. Asters and chrysanthemums had come into their own, and the pebble-dashed house still looked shabby and in need of a coat of paint.

It had not escaped the invasion. Father had done his best and chosen the most suitable evacuees for Mother, but they were an unlikely pair for our draughty house. They were a mother and grown-up daughter, now occupying the spare front bedroom and living with us. They were pleasant and anxious to be no trouble, but my heart sank. Country life was going to be impossible for them. They both wore thin-soled high-heeled shoes and thin fashionable clothes which would never be warm enough to protect them from the Arctic winds which attacked you even going round the side of the house from the front to the back door. Water pipes froze solid there every winter, and there was not even a cold tap indoors.

Mother had no idea how to delegate jobs; it was *her* house and *her* responsibility to run it efficiently. She was constantly trotting and her work seemed to have doubled, chiefly because the evacuees were not used to paraffin lamps and stoves for lighting and cooking, and we still had no bathroom. They felt unable to help her and I doubt if lovely blazing wood fires all day in the sitting room made up to them for our lack of amenities. There was not even a bus going through the village to take them into Harlow, our nearest small town. (The large overspill town for London, Harlow New Town, was not, of course, built until after the war.)

7:    Woodville, my parents' home

Father was able to remove himself from the pressures in the house, because the war gave him the opportunity to use his considerable organising and leadership skills. As an army man, he had spent eleven years in India with the Royal Horse Artillery, where he had met and married my mother. No sooner had they retired to England and the Essex countryside than he was recalled for the Great War, and spent all four years at the front. His parents had been well-to-do Livery Tailors in London, so he was a countryman by adoption. He had been well educated, and was a tall, handsome, reserved man, immaculately dressed when not absorbed with his garden. Then he wore layers of warm, threadbare clothes, a shapeless tweed hat, disgracefully dirty, and a soft wide woollen scarf around his middle with enormous holes in it. My husband inherited this scarf and wore it too, long after my father's death, as if it had some miraculous healing qualities. Mother constantly waged war over these disreputable gardening clothes and annoyed him considerably by giving jackets and old trousers away to tramps, who came begging at the door, when his back was turned.

As well as being the billeting officer for the evacuees, he became Chief Air Raid Warden for the Matching area under Harlow's jurisdiction. Regularly throughout the Second World War he wore the official issue, a thick navy blue

8:    With my parents in the garden at Woodville

9: Local police with Air Raid Wardens from Matching and Harlow.
Father third from left in middle row

siren suit, decorated with the stripes from his war medals, when he was on duty. Communications were difficult in the country then; Father was in the minority in having a telephone. As soon as Harlow Police Station had an Air Raid alert, outlying districts had to be telephoned since they could not hear the sirens. Father then promptly phoned one of his wardens on Matching Green and other small Matching hamlets, if it were possible, before donning his tin hat. This now had pride of place behind the scullery door instead of his Indian topee which had hung there for years and was now relegated to the cupboard under the stairs. He seized the large hand bell, borrowed from the village school, and set off round the village clanging it loudly like a muffin man. It seemed an unnecessary exercise in 1939, but when landmines were dropped, or later Doodle–Bugs rattled across the skies, it was a warning to take cover. As soon as the All Clear was phoned through, he repeated the exercise.

I shall never know why, when he died after the war, I found two small handbells from the church collection among his treasures in the cupboard under the stairs. I sneaked them back to the church and was amazed to find two gaps in the ascending line of handbells on the wall into which these exactly fitted. Had no–one missed them? He must have borrowed them for the duration of the war and forgotten them. Certainly he never used them. They made a feeble ring compared with the resounding noise of the school bell. Perhaps he had them as back–up in case it fell apart at a critical moment.

Evacuees in Matching

10: Air Raid Wardens in Matching with two officers from Harlow
Father second from right on front row

From the beginning of evacuation, children and mothers sent to reception areas near to London quietly packed their bags and returned home. Life in London seemed normal, deceptively safe, the war was phoney and they longed to be back in familiar surroundings. So many of our school children returned from Rochford to Chingford that education was becoming a farce. Teachers protested, too, that it was idiotic to keep us so near to Southend airport.

Another letter arrived from Essex Education Committee. I was needed again. We were all to report back to Wellington Avenue. I wasted no energy on being indignant at being hired and unceremoniously dropped at the Authority's will: I would have a salary again, and G and I could move back into our new home.

We wandered round from room to room, picking up books and wedding presents and touching furniture. G had designed our dining-room furniture, Gordon Russell had interpreted his drawings into working plans, and Chippendale's workshops in the East End had made them for us. We had visited these workshops and chosen each plank of walnut, G rejecting any that he said were too green. He had a craftsman's eye. The first book he ever gave me was *The Wheelwright's Shop*, a classic rare in the thirties, now, I suspect, unobtainable. The resulting furniture was plain and beautifully grained and polished, and solid enough for the table to act as an emergency air-raid shelter in a year or two's time when I dived for cover with a baby in a carrycot. It is still treasured by our eldest daughter in her home.

Essex Education Committee had come up with a new idea. It would not be safe to open the schools for lessons, so we were to work with assignments. Every morning the girls would arrive at nine o'clock, leave the work they had done the previous day to be marked, and take away an alternative exercise book with a new assignment of work we had set. Children had to leave immediately after the exchange; staff could risk their lives and stay on if they choose. Since we had no cars and were not beasts of burden to carry piles of books home with us, we chose to stay. Our ingenuity was taxed to the limit if we were not to bore our pupils with deadly repetitive exercises; we put in hours of preparation, in addition to trying to mark, so that the work was helpful if not very amusing or inspiring. It's not easy to inspire a love of the English language and of English literature by a correspondence course. Some gifted children welcomed the chance to write poems and stories and wallow in books; but the less able the child, the less suitable the system was. They needed me to read poems to them, to introduce them to new books and new ideas, and to stimulate the imagination. I felt bitterly frustrated. I longed for just half-an-hour with each class as it passed rapidly in and out of the school. With text-books giving access to facts and questionnaires, History and Geography teachers found the assignment system more acceptable. However, no-one was persuaded that we were achieving much more than keeping their minds ticking over and occupying them so that they stayed safely at home indoors without driving their mothers to distraction.

Our first Christmas together came and went unremarkably. My mother-in-law and her two spinster sisters came to stay for two nights, duly admired our new home and added little to the jollity of the occasion. I distinctly remember being surprisingly disorganised and feeling very apologetic about it. Anxious to do everything properly, I got out my grandmother's silver cutlery only to find it heavily tarnished and had to spend Christmas Eve cleaning it. Then I buried myself in the kitchen on Christmas morning to make more mince pies, while the three of them sat quietly around the sitting room fire, waiting for the next meal. They hardly knew me and probably regarded me with deep suspicion; I was certainly not in the same league as the Sunday School teacher they had hoped G would marry before he met me.

We worked hard to keep their spirits up that first Christmas, but sighed with relief when they left us and we could go off to Matching. Whatever the weather we walked miles every day. G would also join Father in the woodshed endlessly sawing logs of wood, culled from Matching Wood behind us, just a step from the chickens' run across the ditch. It must be a deeply satisfying chore, watching the saw-dust heap up on the ground while the baskets fill with logs. Affluence has made no difference to our two married sons now: they are equally happy with dead young trees propped across makeshift saw–benches, red in the face with frost and effort, woollen hats pulled down over the ears. It must be inherited: my grandsons are the same. Sawing wood, having magnificent bonfires or sitting on machines to mow the lawn will keep them active in the garden for hours on end. Just so long as no–one suggests that they should do the weeding; and at Christmas time that was neither necessary not possible.

On winter evenings at Matching we curled up and read round the fire, or played a few hands of Bézique or Canasta, Father's favourite card games, and made sure not to miss the news on the wireless. Then we were ready to light our candles and trail up to bed. Nothing had changed at Woodville since I was a child, except the addition of the telephone hanging on the wall in the hall, in a direct draught from the front to the back door. We were all waiting for the changes to come. As 1940 dawned we did not know how dramatic and severe these changes would be.

Chapter III

The Blitz

An official letter arrived for G. He was to present himself for a medical examination. He was obviously fit, a keen rugby player and umpire, used to cycling and walking long distances. He came back from the examination and regaled me with an enlightening account of fastidious doctors lining up a row of naked bodies, instructing them to bend over. (We were naïve enough to think that they were inspecting for worms.) He was passed A1.

This was followed by an offer to train as a pilot in the R.A.F. It had to be a voluntary decision. G did not volunteer, and as it happened, he was never to come into the compulsory age for call-up to the army. We waited for it, but he was already over thirty, and because of his training in industry and in metalwork at college, he was very soon seconded from teaching at Chingford to Walthamstow Technical College to train successive drafts of young raw army recruits in basic mechanics, tool making and maintenance.

Since he wore thick white cotton overalls to work in, I had to wash them to remove the dirt and grease, not a very welcome addition to house work with no washing machine and only a deep butler sink. We learned household chores fast in those days.

I thought G was hard on the army recruits. Many of them, like us, were newly married, others only able to live at home for this short course. They tried arriving late, or pleading sickness, but he insisted on punctuality and no skiving. His job was to turn them out competent to deal with mechanical emergencies, and they had to treat this as serious training. He was right, of course, and not unsympathetic – just not as soft as me.

By June 1940 I was six months' pregnant and finding the daily journey to school on two buses, or the long walk across the forest increasingly tiring, so I handed in my resignation. There was no question of taking maternity leave. Since milk was one of the rationed commodities, mothers-to-be declared their condition to their friendly milkman as early as possible because it meant an extra ration. Three of our children were born during the war and all were healthy well-nourished children. My doctor declared that his patients could be perfectly healthy on rations, although these were tight. We were certainly all slimmer. With some ingenuity and reasonable time I became a good French peasant cook, managing to concoct interesting and acceptable meals with small quantities of essential ingredients by adding herbs or spices and, in savoury dishes, a good selection of home-grown vegetables. They were the real bonus. Allotments came into their own. They were no longer the poor man's garden. Every town had to provide them.

11, 12: Betty & Francis Smith, who shared our home in the Blitz

We acquired two allotments, and although G put such energy into digging that he regularly broke the handles off old tools which Father bequeathed us, he spent all his spare time on them, supplying us throughout the war with all the vegetables we needed. Marmite was easily available to add to stews, and our babies were almost weaned onto thin Marmite sandwiches, or Marmite spread on fingers of toast.

Our garden by the house was sadly neglected. But summer came early in 1940, and having been given four garden chairs as a wedding present, we sat outside under the apple tree on a miserable apology for a lawn. Our closest friends, Betty and Francis, had joined us, and we lazed in the warm sun and watched some larks hovering above, singing joyously. We hardly realised what was happening at first. Then it dawned on us that there were planes glinting in the sun, swooping and dodging in terrible dog–fights, bursting into flames, and there were airman baling out. The men leaped to their feet, pointing out our Spitfires or German Messerschmits. Betty and I sat on in dismay, horrified to watch planes hurtling to the ground and parachutes opening with men dangling from them. It was a riveting spectacle and at first it did not occur to any of us to go indoors for safety. Next morning's papers blazoned the news of The Battle of Britain, a momentous occasion we had witnessed: we were lost in admiration for those skilful and courageous young pilots, and stunned at the awful wastage of our generation.

It was the first realisation too that as civilians we were all going to be involved in this war. In the First World War, our fathers went across the seas; this war came to us. At first London, and particularly London Docks, became the target for the Blitz. By September 1940, sirens wailed every night and although my instinct was to stay upstairs and if necessary come down with the house, wiser advice prevailed and we moved downstairs to the cupboard under the stairs. Often I was alone because G could not get back from Walthamstow if the raid started early. He was supplied with a tin-hat, but buses sometimes stopped early and shrapnel was flying about as Böfors guns trundled up and down the High Road through Buckhurst Hill and Woodford. If he happened to be at home he also took his turn at fire-watching in the area.

We had no Anderson shelter in the garden. I hated the idea; they were cold, damp and cheerless. G bought a very thick wide shelf of wood and fitted it to the length and width of the cupboard under the stairs. We put a mattress on the shelf and another on the floor underneath, though that space was used for stowing the carry-cot after the baby was born. I felt safe there, and allowed for blast by keeping the front, side and back doors on chains: we had learned about the dangers of blast from reports of the Spanish Civil War. Noises of gunfire, landmines thudding, or just doors and windows rattling drove Buster, G's terrier, mad and he raced up and down, barking furiously. My next-door neighbour had an Anderson shelter just outside her back door and it bothered her when I was alone at night, so to please her I would sometimes take the inevitable knitting and sit with her in the shelter. I felt much more vulnerable there.

Some of our friends, older and wealthier, had the most elaborate shelters built, equipped with lighting, food stores and comfortable furniture. One well-to-do neighbour, having despatched his wife and family to a safe area, more or less took up residence in his shelter. His maid complained, when it was noticed that she was obviously pregnant, "I only took him a cup of cocoa!"

Throughout September, the Blitz on London Docks intensified. We were on the suburban outskirts, but as we were surrounded by airfields and gun posts, the noise of guns was incessant, and the red glow over London, as fire bombs rained down destroying vast areas and setting alight warehouses and homes, were terrifying. Every morning the papers and the wireless described the appalling scenes of destruction and paid tribute to the indomitable spirit of the people and the amazing courage of firemen, ambulance men and women, and civilians. London underground stations were opened for night shelters and thousands took their bedding and slept there night after night, building up a camaraderie which made life bearable for the lonely and frightened.

Thousands of families from the dock area had to be evacuated. Some arrived in our area in the night, stunned and silent, in just the clothes they had on, and were given shelter in school rooms and church halls. The church hall across the green from us was full, and before breakfast there was a knock on the door and an urgent request from a voluntary worker –

"How many can you take for breakfast?"

G and I had a family of eight, the parents and six children, shocked and quiet, the light gone out of them; too grateful, so that we felt ashamed not to be suffering with them. Yet they were not complaining: they were alive; many of their friends were dead.

Fortunately my parents had been to see us from Matching a few days previously, a rare event, as transport was difficult; but they had brought fruit from the orchard and fresh eggs from their hens scratching away in Matching Wood. We squandered the dozen on that breakfast. I remembered one of the children sniffing hard and realised they had no handkerchiefs. Paper tissues were unheard of, so without much thought, I produced a pile of neatly folded handkerchiefs from my sachet upstairs and distributed them round to each. I shall never know if that was a deeply embarrassing thing to do. G said afterwards that they probably didn't use handkerchiefs, and I remembered the village children of my youth who only used torn rag. They took them gracefully; I hope they didn't feel patronised and insulted.

Cooking facilities were set up in the church halls and there was no shortage of voluntary workers. Some families were found homes in empty houses and stayed with us in Buckhurst Hill for many years. Just then their needs were great. Another knock on the door; this time it was for coats and blankets. Everyone gave generously; no-one kept two coats if one was needed. Because I was pregnant, solicitous friends turned down all my offers of help at these centres in case of infection. I was feeling remarkably fit in spite of chronic loss of sleep, but they were adamant.

At Matching many of the original evacuees, including my parents' mother and daughter, had returned to London. However, Woodville was fuller than ever. The Rev. J.B. Brinkworth and his wife and daughter, well-known to us from my childhood, had now retired from Matching vicarage and gone to live at Woodford Green, where Dora, their daughter and my former music teacher, was in partnership with Tommy Farrell, a chiropodist. When the Blitz became intolerable they wrote to my mother and asked her if she would have them as paying guests. There was no way my mother would have them as paying guests, but she was delighted to have them as guests. I suspect they would have been happier to have kept to their suggestion, but there was no arguing with my mother.

The vicar and his wife moved into a spare bedroom and lived with my parents. Every morning Tommy and Dora drove to Woodville for the night and back to Woodford Green each morning.

As I grew visibly more pregnant and G was not often at home at night, they plotted together to persuade me that I should travel out with them each evening and at least sleep peacefully in the country. It was my duty to myself and the baby. I gave in, but not without a protest.

I looked forward to a sound sleep in my old bed. However the first night I was there, Father was out clanging his school bell. An Alert was on. We all nonchalantly stayed in bed, but Father on his return was not going to allow this, and until the All Clear and his final tramp round the Tye, we sat around in the dining-room, resuscitated the log fire and chatted quietly.

I continued to live in two places for a week or two, but I wanted to go back to G, and to make arrangements for the birth or our baby. Betty was also pregnant with her first baby and we were due within a week or two of each other. Francis had become G's best friend when he was a graduate student at ASEA and G was earning money for college there. We have remained close friends ever since and both families have two boys and two girls, all within the same age range. Our mutual doctor half suspected competition!

While we were back in our cupboard under the stairs, their flat in Walthamstow suffered bomb damage and they came to live with us. We had a side hall at right-angles to the main hall with our cupboard under the stairs, so they fitted it with a mattress and bedded down there each night. It was quite a cosy arrangement for Betty and me when our husbands were working or fire-watching, or in Francis' case, acting as a medical orderly at the hospital.

Our concern was for the immediate future; where to have our babies and how to get there safely. Every night from September to November in 1940 the sirens started undulating as soon as it was dark; within a very short time enemy bombers throbbed across the Channel and the horrendous Blitz continued on London and on towns on the South coast too. Neither we nor friends near us had cars, and public transport was understandably unreliable. We would like to have gone further into the country, not closer to London. I had wild ideas, and wrote to a recently married District Nurse from Matching who was living on Hatfield Heath to see if she would consider taking us in as maternity patients. She may have thought it impertinent. She wrote back turning the suggestion down and assuring me cheerfully that all would be well and to book in locally. I don't expect she had any idea what it was like to live so close to London under a constant alert, and decided she was dealing with two frightened first-time mothers.

We had to take a risk. We both booked into the nearest Nursing Home at Woodford Green for two consecutive fortnights in November. I marvel now at the speed with which young mothers come back home with their babies within twenty-four hours of birth; we lazed and treated the fortnight as a holiday from tough household chores.

There was an Alert, but no local bombing during the night my baby was born. We had ordered a taxi, so G and I quietly abandoned the cupboard, picked up the case we had already packed and left for the last week downstairs, and arrived at Woodside Nursing Home within ten minutes. It is now an old people's home; then it was small, professionally run, and each of us luxuriated in single rooms. I was so green about the whole procedure that I did exactly as I was told, swallowing revolting cod liver oil floating on orange juice with only a grimace and having a totally unnecessary hot bath. There was no suggestion that G should stay with me; the staff would have thrown up their hands in horror, and strange as it may seem, I preferred it that way. We were all brought up on lovely romantic ideas; and I only wanted him to arrive clutching flowers when I was propped up, looking pale and sentimental, powdered and scented, in a charming bed-jacket with a beshawled baby tucked in my arms, the messy business over. It didn't quite turn out like that because the babies had to be taken away from us and kept in a basement shelter. I was afraid that he would go down and coo over the wrong baby, and since we were poor, the flowers he brought were rather battered chrysanthemums plucked from our dismal garden. It never occurred to me to doubt that the baby would be perfect; it was a boy, only five and a half pounds, and nurse stuck his ears back with sticking plaster because they had been bent forward at birth. We were besotted with him.

Matron was charming, but Sister was impressive, elderly and brooking no nonsense. She informed me that she had brought hundreds of babies into the world and her methods were infallible. She insisted on wrapping each baby up like a little mummy, pulling the shawl so tightly round that no arms could escape and wave about. Loose arms made them restless, she said. Nor could he turn over, so at regular intervals you turned him from one side to the other like a turkey in the oven. I went along with her methods a little dubiously, but they seemed to work: the baby slept peacefully and prospered.

Betty in her turn, a week or two later, rebelled. She was not made of such gullible material. She had started training as a nurse at the London Hospital after a degree course in mathematics at Bedford College, but had resigned and married Francis as war broke out. She challenged some of Sister's decisions; it was her baby (also a boy and also called John), and she was in charge. Sister was furious and took an instant dislike to her, commenting to me,

"She's no nurse! The ink never dried on her certificate, I know."

But Betty won. Our respective sons thrived and our doctor pulled our legs, protesting that he never knew which husband belonged to which. That confusion was solved when Betty and Francis bought a new home a short distance away from us. When we returned home the local authority provided us with a baby's version of the gas mask. This was a bulky cardboard coffin with a plastic top; impossible to imagine a baby's reaction to being shut away from its parents inside it. Fortunately it was never used.

Chapter IV

A Baby with Whooping Cough

Sleep was doomed to be broken. If we were not leaping up because of an Alert, we were trying to pacify a presumably hungry baby. There was no feeding on demand then; we just struggled with a little warm water and sugar to span the gap to the next four-hourly feed. For a small baby, John had remarkable lungs. I had spent three weeks in the Nursing Home because of mastitis and feeding problems and returned home to the exhausting routine of expressing breast milk, weighing the baby at every feed and topping up with a bottle of Cow and Gate, which he was prone to reject. I was frustrated and G was often absent at College.

Once more Mother came to the rescue. She was experienced in all these matters, having set up and run a Baby Welfare Clinic at Matching for Essex County Council for many years. So, the Brinkworth's having now returned to Woodford during a lull in night attacks, I once more returned to Woodville. Mother was indefatigable; I realise now how utterly selfless she was. She installed me with the baby in a front bedroom, kept a coal fire burning in the grate there, trailed up and down stairs with hot water for bathing the baby, and gave me breakfast in bed every morning. She must have been exhausted, but never complained. The baby and I flourished. Within a couple of weeks we were fit and rearing to go, so we left Woodville to settle down to a short period of calm, and returned to Buckhurst Hill and G.

We had scoured advertisements in the local papers and found a second-hand pram for sale. It was rather a long way beyond Woodford, near the Napier Arms, but quite undaunted we proudly pushed it all the way home. It was just what we wanted, a kind rarely seen in these days of flimsy pushchairs and plastic hoods. We washed and polished it and there it was; white-lined, tall, boat-shaped, padded and beautifully sprung. It lasted another ten years and was used by all our four children, getting yearly more shabby. Come rain or snow they slept outdoors in it in the daytime. I had a fetish for fresh air; snow up to the top of the wheels was no hindrance. My doctor thoroughly approved. When they woke up there were leaves dancing on the apple tree above them, or a yellow forsythia hedge beside them; much more entertaining than the ceiling above a cot.

Strange as it may seem, my country childhood was almost too healthy. I missed out on most infectious diseases then, so I succumbed to them later with my children: mumps, which hardly affected them or their appetites, completely

13:    Edgar & Hilda Tinney by the pram

14:    John in the pram at Woodville.
From the left: Father, me, Mother, G, my sister Ruth, and her daughter Shirlie

knocked me down so that I could hardly swallow and looked as if I had been blown up with a bicycle pump; chicken-pox when my younger son was only three months old, covering me and him with a prolific rash of beastly blistered spots; and now when John was not quite six months old, the whooping cough.

Our kind neighbours were really worried. In my ignorance, it never entered my head to think it might be fatal in such a young baby. There was no vaccination for whooping cough then, though the three later children all benefited from it. A small baby, he was only just reaching his normal weight and, due to the encouragement of the "infallible" Sister, was now bottle-fed. It was a struggle for him to keep down any food, and paroxysms of the peculiar, frightening, cough shook his small frame. With supreme confidence, I calmly devoted most of my time to him. Only once I asked the doctor if he would be all right, and his reply, "Yes, I think so, now," made me realise that he had ever doubted it. Fresh air was my panacea for all sickness. So back to Woodville I went to let Matching finish the healing.

Whenever we visited our parents with babies, my sister and I always borrowed a pram from our great friend and farming neighbour, Hilda Tinney at Housham Hall. Since her children were now away at school, the pram was a distinctly old-fashioned affair. It was deep and square-looking, a

15:    Matching Church, with the Marriage Feast Room in front

mud-coloured Dunkley, invaluable for energetic babies because it was too heavy to turn over, but that was not a problem at the moment. We all found it a hilarious object, but very useful.

Every day I set off from Matching Tye and walked miles with John in the pram, stopping to support him when the cough overtook him, lulling him off to sleep with the movement in between bouts. It was the end of April 1941 and spring was in full swing; some primroses and 'peggles' lingered in the ditches; violets, light and dark purple, were almost hidden as the grass grew taller. There was even an occasional clump of oxslips. I had almost forgotten their existence, but they peppered the meadows when I was a child there in the Twenties.

I kept to the roads, gravelled then but tarmacked now, from the Tye to Matching Green, past the Women's Institute Hall and the Chapel next door where I had spent so many Sunday afternoons and evenings, and leaving the wood behind on the right, passed the Round House, now transformed from a poverty-stricken cottage to a desirable house with smart additions dwarfing its original shape.

There was no lingering on the Green. If it was to be a circular tour I had to press on, sometimes turning immediately right, or if I was not feeling so energetic, continuing on the left of the Green and leaving it behind after the blacksmith's shop.

16: Hogg's Farm

Turning right I followed the lonely road passing High Laver Grange. The garden was always spectacular, lawns meeting the pond by the roadside, primulas and wallflowers massed on its banks. It was a working farm owned by the Gemmells. Cows streamed across the road from the meadow to the cowsheds to be milked, their legs filthy from the churned-up mud in the gateway, dropping clods as they nudged each other across.

I bumped the old pram over the clods, turning right towards Magdalen Laver opposite High Laver Hall and the track to the church where John Locke is buried; then right again towards Matching down Faggoters' Lane. It was all familiar ground, cottages and farms far apart, but many still with families I knew. I often made a last call at Hogg's Farm, not very flourishing when I was a child, but now white-washed and smart. Frank Fenton, now married, lived there. He used to live at Shetlocks Farm opposite Woodville when we were all children together, sharing a tennis court in the meadow beside us which had to be rolled every day since moles threw up dozens of heaps during the night, accounting, so we claimed, for our lack of skill.

We disturbed a ridiculous column of waddling white ducks as we passed and they tumbled over themselves in their hurry to reach the safety of the pond. Every farm had a pond for the farm horses to lumber down to at the end of the day; but already primitive tractors with no shelter to protect the driver were clattering around the stack yards. Even the stack yards with their rows of thatched circular piles of wheat sheaves were giving way to gawky Dutch barns, their bright red corrugated-iron roofs held high on tall legs slashing the landscape. They were a brash intrusion in the green and earth-coloured countryside.

It was good to catch up with Matching Wood again. Bluebells were nearly over, but orchids and lady's slippers stood out where the undergrowth was cleared. May trees still held their flowers tightly closed against cold winds, black ash buds had only just broken, but oaks uncurled light-brown leaves, and red sycamores had burst into points.

Some mornings when I reached Matching Green on my daily pram-pushing therapy I followed the road to Hatfield Heath, taking the narrow lane to Matching Church, past Sister Rushworth's house on the corner. This led past the spinney of tall fir trees, already sadly denuded for pit-props and not replaced with young trees as they were no longer needed in this age of steel and concrete. Behind it lay the famous Lily Pond, devoid of lilies now, but the boat house was there and the water still slipped down a small grilled cascade and under the road. A place to linger. It was tough pushing the pram up the hill to the church where G and I had married two years before, past the Marriage Feast Room overhanging a cottage and the new road sign prohibiting vehicles and

17:    The John Howards' home, Matching Hall

Chapter IV

reminding us that it was a private road. We had not met such restrictions before. Old John Howard still lived at Matching Hall behind the duck pond. I only stopped to nose around the ancient cart sheds beside the road, and pulled out a "poker" from the rushes choking the pond in front of the groom's house lower down the hill.

It was a long haul now and rough underfoot; a time to pause at the Byford's cottage to admire the garden and catch up on village gossip. Further on the shouts and noises proclaimed playtime at the village school, almost unaltered since I was a five–year–old starting school there in 1918: the same high windows and bleak playground.

A mile further on and I was back on the Tye and Woodville sheltering by the wood.

A week or so later the whooping cough had almost subsided, John was beginning to feed normally and trying to sit up. The country had done its healing job. I made plans to return home to G. It was May and a wrench to leave the countryside. Meadows were alight with buttercups and daisies, verges studded with patches of red and white campions and cow–parsley waist high on either side of the road, filling the air with its heavy smell, leaning in the rain, lace–like in the sun. Arable fields were bright green with spikes of wheat. Cuckoos called urgently from the wood. Thrushes and warblers competed in bursts of song. I packed multitudes of nappies, turned my back on eggs fresh from the nest, and returned to Buckhurst Hill to battle with packets of dried eggs and rather more involvement in household chores.

Chapter V

Coping with Rations

I can mislay scissors with the greatest of ease. Shopkeepers throughout the war, and while rationing lasted afterwards, were models of efficiency. I never saw one hunt frantically for scissors. They always seemed readily to hand, often tied to an apron or overall with a piece of string; they were essential for cutting off small rectangles in groups or strips from the ration books we carried everywhere, getting steadily more dog-eared, but providing us with all basic commodities.

We had registered for ration books as soon as war broke out, but rationing did not begin until January 1940, and Lord Woolton was not appointed Minister of Food until March of that year. Then the rationing of all staple foods was in earnest, quantities becoming more stringent as the war dragged on and shipping was a target for enemy planes and submarines.

I had three ration books: two buff-coloured for adults and one green for baby John while under five. This allowed him a daily pint of milk, half an adult ration of meat and twice an adult egg ration. In winter months adults had only one egg every two months, but in the laying season sometimes three or four eggs a week; luxury indeed. Every two months we had the bonus of a packet of dried eggs, the equivalent of twelve eggs. It sounds revolting, but it was possible to transform it into passable scrambled eggs; usually it was used for making the occasional cake or pudding, so long as enough sugar had been saved from the ration (which varied from half a pound to three-quarters a week) and fat had been saved up from the very meagre ration of between two to four ounces. A birthday party could cripple menus for a month; but usually all the family and friends co-operated. On a visit you took your ration of tea and sugar with you.

By June 1940 news on the wireless was disquietening. Belgium had capitulated and France was overrun by Germans. Our troops were marooned on the mainland with practically no equipment left, and had to be evacuated home to England as soon as possible. They were retreating towards Dunkirk, and from East Anglia and the South coast the strangest motley collection of small ships set off to rescue them. Most of us knew someone involved.

Private yachts, small sailing boats, fishing boats, seaside pleasure boats, many of them tackling the longest and most dangerous trip of their life, set off from small ports and holiday resorts around the coast to pick up our troops, desperate to get away. It was a drama to thrill us all had we not been so concerned with the urgency of the operation.

Churchill's sonorous voice, which had earlier moved us with his "blood, sweat and tears" speech, once more came on the air and made his famous speech assuring us that we would "fight on the beaches, on the landing grounds, in the fields, in the streets and on the hills". It is probably difficult for young people today to realise the tremendous impact of his rhetoric, but it caught the imagination of the ordinary man and woman. The "Dunkirk spirit" was aroused and unquenchable; he inspired us with supreme confidence in his ability to lead us to a victorious outcome of this war, which at the time appeared to be threatening defeat.

From July 1940, after Dunkirk and the German occupation of France, rations tightened. Tea was only two ounces a week. G's mother, like all people living alone, viewed this with dismay, and was hard pressed to make hers spin out; but we could usually help as we preferred weak tea, a pale beverage my sister Ruth rudely referred to as "winkle–wash". It was surprising how many of us discovered we could easily do without sugar in hot drinks and have never gone back to using it since. Fat was more difficult and like many other mothers I occasionally made a sponge cake with liquid paraffin, until we were warned against such a practice as medically unsound.

In these days when we eat all kinds of wholemeal and wheatmeal bread it is difficult to believe that the introduction of a national loaf of bread made from whole grain, and the sudden demise of the white load, was regarded as a minor tragedy. It was dull, grey, and speckled, and disliked. However it was filling and rationed only by its steadily rising price. Fish and offal were off the ration, but they became scarce and price prohibited them as a regular source of protein. Queues formed immediately the news got round that a scarce or luxury food was available. I rarely joined one. Luxury foods were not for us. In fact sweet rationing was not a problem; we could not afford to buy the family ration and were able to give some coupons away to our friends. Fruit was essential, but oranges and bananas were a luxury, and the children refused to eat them at the end of the war because they were unfamiliar. It took many attempts to persuade John to eat anything so ridiculously shaped as a banana.

I was lucky because I had access to plenty of soft fruit in season and a surfeit of plums and apples from my parents' orchard at Matching. Mother's pantry was full of bottled fruit and jars of preserves. In the weekends before I married she insisted on helping me to make a supply of jam, chutneys, and lemon curd with a quantity of fresh eggs warm from the nest. We all had cause to bless her help and foresight. There were fresh red and blackcurrants galore, loganberries and raspberries too, just so long as my parents remained at Woodville and that was until the end of the war though not until the end of rationing, which lingered on for another seven years.

18:    Anne Bury as a bridesmaid

19:    John in clothes made from mine

There was a British Restaurant on the High Road in Buckhurst Hill which was invaluable for older people and for those living on their own. It provided a good nourishing meal of meat and two veg. very cheaply; and meat and two veg. was the only acceptable dinner for many people. Fortunately Mother had not brought up Ruth and me to be conservative about food. We enjoyed experimenting with odd remnants of food and G's allotment vegetables could be served in many guises: in stews, batters made with dried eggs, cheese and potato cakes, rissoles with a minimum of minced meat, and bowls of hot broth. The butcher had bones to sell cheaply, and all my children were easily weaned onto bone and vegetable broth. A stock–pot was our salvation.

In 1941 clothes were rationed on a point system. This never bothered us either: we simply could not afford to use them up. Old friends were delighted when we could give them clothes coupons, particularly unmarried colleagues who were used to dressing well.

Anne, a close friend since our years together at Homerton College, Cambridge, in the early thirties, now teaching at Liverpool, arrived at frequent intervals to collect coupons. We enjoyed her visits; tall, with strikingly handsome features causing heads to turn, she would stride in at short notice, fitting into the family as easily as if she had only been away on a short shopping foray. We were her family; she was the children's indulgent and invaluable "spinster" aunt. Her parents, cotton mill–owners in Blackburn, were both dead, and from all accounts had been strict non–conformists unable to demonstrate affection either to each other or to their children. Her only brother, Fred, was reading mathematics at Cambridge when war broke out and after one year, like so many of his contemporaries, he had joined up and was now an officer in the Air Force.

She settled in, cheered us up with accounts of the young scalliwags she taught and obviously understood and liked, and bossed us about until we rebelled. We blessed her for the books she brought us, argued fiercely about politics and religion, and took a lively interest in the elegant clothes she bought with our coupons.

I was lucky to be small. Usually I moaned at the disadvantages: mirrors too high, shelves out of reach. Now I came into my own. My richer friends regularly passed on to me their fashionable suits and dresses in excellent condition so that I could adjust them or cut them up for something else. Mother had given me her original old Singer Sewing machine, a very heavy black affair with gold decoration, worked by hand. No matter; it had plenty of life left in it and with demonstrations and some advice from Mother, I was able to make passable clothes for myself and throughout the war for my children. I made all John's shirts and short linen pants from old frocks and skirts, and the *pièce-de-résistance* was his first siren-suit with a hood, made from my dog's-tooth tweed overcoat. It was not a very professional-looking affair, but it was warm and comfortable and held together throughout the winter of 1943.

An evening dress presented greater difficulties; but a chance to wear one was not to be missed. The Blitz of 1940 was followed in 1941 with the Battle of the Atlantic. Although this meant tighter rationing, it was preferable to sleepless bomb-disturbed nights. We even felt we dared to accept an invitation and leave our son in bed in charge of a sitter-in. The Tinneys of Housham Hall, my friends from childhood in Matching, were giving a Supper Dance at Long's Restaurant in Bishop's Stortford to celebrate the Twenty-First birthday of their only son, Clifford. All their farmer friends from miles around would be there; we couldn't bear to miss it. But how to get there? And what to wear?

Luckily G shared a dinner suit with his brother, Rob; but the dress I had made before the war from a pattern meticulously measured and cut by G on the living-room floor was no longer whole. I had fallen in love with a Schiaparelli design in a glossy magazine – a navy blue taffeta bolero and full long skirt split down the front, worn over a delicate pale pink organdie frock. I thought it was a dream. G had used all his mathematical skills to draw out this skirt of many panels so that it would fit closely at the waist, but swirl into yards round the bottom. He had knelt on the floor with paper and rule and had finally dared to cut it out. I had made a simple organdie under-frock and sewn the taffeta outfit together on the old Singer before sending it off to be picot-edged at Bourne and Hollingsworth in New Oxford Street.

But now the under-frock was no more and the navy was fast losing its depth of colour. New materials and money were scarce; but we were determined to go. The Tinneys had laid on transport; farmer friends in Upshire would pick us up and deposit us home again. We surveyed my outfit; definitely turning mauve in places, but it had to do. So I sewed it all together, joining the skirt together and turning the bolero into the bodice. A strip left over made a wide belt and covered up most of the damage. It looked depressingly dull. It needed some white to create a contrast. Sacrilege it may have been, but I tracked down some white suede. Father, an Essex Provincial Grand Swordbearer of the Freemasons, had a discarded Masonic apron which gloried in a white suede background. I cut and joined two strips of it and slashed vertical cuts along the middle portion through which I threaded the navy sash, making a very effective cummerbund. Then I turned my attention to a pair of Mother's long white kid evening gloves, leftovers from more gracious days in India and far too narrow for me to wear, and made a flower for my shoulder. No longer a Schiaparelli design, but if you ignored the faded bits, quite a smart outfit.

We had a lovely evening; a highlight in an otherwise bleak year.

Chapter VI

Evacuees in Buckhurst Hill

Suddenly the church bells stopped. G and I missed them waking us up on Sunday mornings since the parish church of St. John's was opposite us, across the Green, at Buckhurst Hill. This was 1940 and they would not ring again until they announced that the war was over.

Signposts disappeared in order to mislead any odd German who dared to parachute down in our midst. Town people were completely confused when they ventured into the countryside. For four years G and I only moved on familiar ground; visits to Matching and a very occasional trip to Suffolk and my mother's relations who were still alive. Lack of signposts though would not bother a country child, for roads there constantly ended in a T–junction with no indication which way to turn.

Monstrous bulging animal–like objects now became a feature of the landscape. Barrage Balloons floated above the trees near the river Roding, in the valley between Buckhurst Hill and Chigwell. They were tethered to the ground like blown–up walruses and could be highered or lowered at will, since they were designed to entangle enemy aircraft if they flew in low towards the City. We regarded them with friendly disbelief.

From 1940 onwards, all of us kept stirrup pumps, buckets of water and sand–bags at the ready. In London during the Blitz they were little more than a gesture, since three million homes were damaged and over thirty thousand lost their lives. Firemen were among the bravest and most exhausted members of the community; fire bombs rained down to light up the area for enemy bombing. The bombs were not selective: churches, homes, schools and shops were all damaged. Gas and water mains were hit, electricity destroyed and sewers exposed. Thousands of evacuees now had no choice but to leave London; waves of them moved out after each raid. Most of them wanted to go no further than the suburbs; both men and women had to get to their work as all but the old and sick were enlisted in the war effort.

Every available hall in Buckhurst Hill was commandeered and designated as a Rest Centre. There was never a lack of volunteers to help. The official mind envisaged the Centres as transitory stops for the homeless until they found more suitable accommodation: no–one was to be encouraged to stay too long in case the families lost the initiative to help themselves and become apathetic. The women were wonderful, struggling to prevent their surroundings from degenerating into squalor. Most of the burden fell on them since the men were either at the war, in factories or Civil Defence. They had the children, the old and frail and the handicapped to look after and comfort. On top of this they searched for homes and queued at shops, often having to go through all the frustrating bureaucracy of getting new issues of ration books at unfamiliar offices and re–registering at new shops. The women rarely ate their full rations, but made sure that their charges were satisfied.

Public air raid shelters were put up; one on the Green on the other side of the road; with a bench round inside the walls. Few people used them. They were almost as dark and unsavoury as an Anderson shelter in the back garden; perhaps not so inclined to flood after a rain, but equally damp and smelly.

I put an advertisement in the local paper for help in the house twice a week. It sounds pretty feeble now. I felt I was not coping well enough with quite a big house, very few modern appliances, and a new baby. During the following ten years I managed to cope with four children, three under six at one time, and two grandmothers at loggerheads living with us, with ever–decreasing help and finally none at all, so it must have been merely a matter of acclimatisation to a domestic role and loss of sleep.

Actually the advertisement brought us the greatest piece of good fortune. Mrs Harris became our guardian angel. She and her husband, both in their late sixties, were bombed out of London, came to the Rest Centre in the church hall and soon set about making a home in a large old empty house on the Epping New Road. She was a treasure. She was comfortably built, had rather frizzy hair, and shuffled on her "bad feet", changing into bedroom slippers to work. When she unwrapped her clean overall, she was ready to tackle anything. With a sardonic sense of humour she cut a swathe through my life, tidying up, washing out nappies, bringing up wind and restoring calm and order wherever she went. She not only removed the heavy work from my shoulders, she entertained me hugely.

Monday was her day. On Sunday she had wallowed in the *People* and the *News of the World*, and over a protracted coffee break she regaled me with the latest scandals and court cases. It became a pattern. G and I took the *Observer*, if we bothered with a Sunday paper. The wireless was our source of news, almost entirely geared to the war effort and reports of our armies and convoys. I'm sure Mrs Harris listened too, but rarely mentioned such matters. With a horrified relish she recited the salacious details to me from her Sunday papers, tossing her head and wondering what the world was coming to. Bombs might obliterate Hackney, fire devour the very street she had lived in, but equally outrageous to her were the divorces and loose behaviour of totally unknown folk with which the reporters sought to liven up her Sunday reading. Her weekend dose became like a fix; she saved up the tastiest morsels to retell me. I think she realised that she was a great source of amusement and weekly polished her wit as a raconteur.

Suddenly she would stop, scramble to her feet, sweep the cups into the sink and complain that she was wasting time and must get on. By lunch time when she was due to leave, she inevitably said,

"If you find me a bite of lunch to eat, I'll stay on and wash out that batch of clothes."

I would remind her that she had done her allotted time –

"No matter. I'm not going to leave you with that pile. I don't want no more money."

She must have gone home with aching feet, but was always cheerful. We were her family and she had to put us straight; then her satisfaction was complete. I had no washing machine, so it meant starting after lunch to tackle the clothes by hand in an old–fashioned Butler sink. She took this in her stride and insisted on pegging it all out on the line in the garden. Kind and supportive, she always went the "extra mile", for which I could never have afforded to pay. I had the best of the bargain, and was grateful. She and her family had lost everything in the Blitz, yet she never complained about her personal troubles. She was glad to be alive and well.

We always amused her by calling her Shah. When John began to talk he had the greatest difficulty in saying Mrs Harris, and for a long time the nearest he could manage was Shah. So Shah she affectionately remained.

Chapter VII

A Sudden Birth

Austerity increased in 1942. All ranges of furniture, china and household goods were made in a utility range only. White cups and saucers, not unfortunately "blue-ringed" as Rupert Brooke loved, were the only choice; plain light dining-room tables and chairs with much substitution of plywood in cupboards; and almost no curtain materials. For years I bought plain dress material, much too narrow, for bedroom curtains.

G and I were lucky; we had bought all the furniture we really needed just before the outbreak of war. Many of our friends, hastily marrying now, were not so lucky.

Gaps among our friends were increasing too; many of the young men who had joined the air force with such excitement were reported missing. Younger brothers of friends called to see us in their new fighter pilot uniform, having left Cambridge at the end of their first year. Some of them were to go back at the end of the war to finish their degrees, no longer jaunty and irresponsible, but sober men thankful to be alive, with closed compartments behind their eyes. They reminded me of my father, who had spent four years at the Front in the First World War, and would never talk about it. Sometimes Mother said he woke with nightmares, always at the War; but if old comrades looked him up for a chat, he could never be drawn to reminisce; it was a closed book: he stared into the fire and answered in unrevealing monosyllables.

In East Anglia, as elsewhere, the War Agricultural Committee was hard at work encouraging farmers to utilise every scrap of spare land. Never was the countryside so tidy and productive. Edgar Tinney from Housham Hall was a member of the "War Ag.", as it was known, driving backwards and forwards to Chelmsford, planning, advising less successful farmers, and pushing himself towards an early fatal heart attack. Yet he found time to come out to Buckhurst Hill occasionally to bring us sacks of peas or potatoes.

To alleviate the black-out in the winter, Essex County Education Committee set up evening classes and, anxious to escape interminable nappies and bottles, I agreed to take a Drama class for Buckhurst Hill Community Centre; I was also grateful for the money. Anyone who has worked on County classes knows the concern to keep up numbers at every class or it is summarily threatened with closure; mine was no exception, and catching buses in the blackout was no great fun. However G took over at home for one night a week and the class began to flourish at the County High School in spite of dark empty corridors and a stage in a vast assembly hall. In the following years, it was much

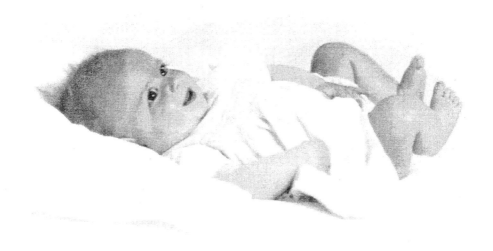

20:    Diana: "She was born wise"

more fun to use smaller venues closer to home and best of all was to put on outdoor performances during the summer.

Walter Spradbury, a well known artist married to Dorothy D'Orsay, the opera singer and friend of Ethel Smythe, lived near us at The Wilderness. They had tamed the lawns in one area and created a grassy outdoor stage. Dorothy had a room in the house, smelling slightly musty, but containing one grand piano and a quantity of large trunks. It was an Aladdin's cave of theatrical costumes of all kinds. She could be guaranteed to dress any cast in clothes for any period, many costumes having been bought when she was busy with her tireless energy putting on musical evenings and light operas in the garden. She allowed us all to riffle through the trunks and extract clothes, fans, yards of lace and accessories. A regular washing, ironing and airing was good for them. Soon I was involved in the Spradbury Familys' community work and I put on several of Lady Gregory's short plays in the garden.

Meanwhile the wireless kept us jolly with Workers' Playtime. This programme of concerts given in factories during the lunch hour attracted all the well-known bands and comedians. We were inseparable from our wirelesses during the length of the war. The BBC was invaluable for news and Government notices and exhortations, but it also provided most of our entertainment: we hated to miss our dose of Much Binding in the Marsh, Itma and Round the Horn.

The wireless shocked us too. With television now we are used to seeing violence, devastating pictures of famine victims, children dying in whimpering misery: sometimes so many sights that our imaginations and sensibilities are blunted. Only sounds hit us during the war. I can still hear the crying and screaming of babies in despair when Greece was drawn into the war. We were outraged and helpless.

John was now fifteen months old, a healthy, busy child; and I was pregnant again. The baby was born a week after John's second birthday in November 1942. My mother had already arrived to take over the household. Fortunately the war was quiet. Quite suddenly around midnight I awoke to find "the water had broken": the baby had decided to arrive quickly.

The only warm place in the house was by the kitchen-cum-living room fire, so I traipsed downstairs in my dressing gown intending to dress there. G, wide awake and not visibly perturbed at a possible crisis, was entirely in command of the situation. He disappeared to use a friend's phone a few doors away to call an ambulance, warn the Nursing Home of my imminent arrival, and alert our doctor to meet me there. Mother, aroused from her bed, walked helplessly up and down begging me not to have it yet. I was past caring and well into frequent spasms of fierce pain. I knelt on the floor in front of the fire, folded my arms on a chair seat with my head resting on them and roared loudly. I remember thinking that this was being a primitive woman and must be the peasant blood in me. Mother, wringing her hands, "Darling, please don't have it here!" G, on his return, cheerfully encouraging, "Go right ahead dear. You have it as soon as you can."

I had no ability to choose between the conflicting advice. A nurse neighbour popped in, slipped a clean towel under me and put the kettle on. Our sturdy eight and a half pound baby was promptly born on the kitchen floor.

Mother was horrified; this was no way to behave. G disappeared to the phone again to cancel his previous arrangements; the doctor must come to the house.

Within a short while he was with us. Dr Foster-Smith was a great friend of our family doctor in Matching; a solid, middle-aged man, kind and sensible and utterly dependable, a tremendous support to G and me throughout our family life. He never refused to visit in the years to come and could be contacted for advice on the phone at any time: a real friend. He took in the situation at a glance, promptly cut the cord which cheered my mother who had been really bothered about it, examined the placenta, wrapped up the baby, patted me on the shoulder, and against his better judgement, allowed me a much-desired cup of tea.

The ambulance arrived. I was carried out and set off alone. Mother had to stay because of John who had slept peacefully through the drama, and G with the baby in his arms, wrapped up in a thick shawl, proudly followed with the doctor in his car. The nursing home was fully alerted. The same Sister was there, hustling the ambulance men.

"Do hurry! Mrs Collecott will be quick now." I giggled.

"Don't worry, Sister. G's bringing the baby in."

"Don't be ridiculous!" she admonished me severely. This was no time to be frivolous. Her face froze in disbelief as I explained the situation.

It was not yet all over. I had been badly torn with a too-sudden birth and the doctor had to stitch me up.

"I'd rather you managed without an anaesthetic," he said kindly. "You'll feel so much better afterwards." I consented with a gay ignorance, but was glad when it was all over and I was allowed to sleep.

Diana, our beautiful daughter, had made her first firm statement. She had set the pattern of her life. A friend, bending over her cot, later commented,

"She's born wise."

Chapter VIII

The Americans in Matching

During 1943 G was relieved of teaching raw army recruits and posted back to school, at first in his old job in Chingford, and later to a similar, but co-educational, school in Loughton. This was much more convenient and, since he was taking evening classes as well, it meant that he could come home to tea and help bath the children between sessions.

Youth Centres came into their own during the war. Loughton had a flourishing one under Pearl Newman, a delightful young teacher who was also the Warden. When he was not taking evening classes, G was appointed as Assistant Warden to her. We became great friends.

Pearl was a widow after only a few months' marriage. Her husband, Jack, was tragically killed while army training on night manoeuvres. He was leading a group of soldiers and jumped over a wall in the dark; there was an unexpected deep drop on the other side and he was killed. Pearl was a remarkable girl and coped with her grief by throwing herself into activity: she was a most popular Warden, particularly with the youths waiting for call-up. They found her sympathetic and tough, organising football teams and matches and providing a friendly social atmosphere at the Centre.

21:   Loughton School Staff. G fourth from left on back row

By the summer Allied troops were on the continent and Italy had surrendered. More and more American troops were arriving in England, particularly in East Anglia. Many were stationed in Suffolk and inside the Essex borders. We were delighted to see them: they were young, cheerful, and healthy-looking men. Secretly we thought them less smart than our own soldiers: their socks were wrinkled and they wore ties. (Only officers wore ties in the British forces). Rumours abounded about the vast quantities of food, including mandatory ice-cream, which accompanied them everywhere; unheard of luxuries for us, but necessities for them. We were convinced they were spoilt, but they were friendly and generous and their popularity was never in question. They made themselves at home, and the number of GI brides from East Anglia is proof enough of their warm welcome in village communities.

Matching Green was only one of at least ten new airfields now coming into use in this part of Essex. They stretched from Boreham near Chelmsford to Earls Colne near Colchester, springing up in Gosfield, Great Saling, Easton Lodge, Little Walden, Rivenhall, Wethersfield, Stansted and Willingale; and in Matching Green on the road to the Rodings. Each aerodrome was soon to become home to the United States 9th Air Force, flying light and medium Marauder bombers.

So urgent had been the need for airfields in Europe by May, 1942, that Engineer Battalions were shipped from the United States with all their relevant equipment. At Matching their assignment was to build a full-scale three-runway aerodrome with all the necessary hangars, buildings and utilities for this to function. Since Matching still had not the most basic facilities, this was a major undertaking. From 1942 to 1944 the Matching aerodrome took fifteen months to build.

"Up the road" from the Green, a large area of rich farmland, owned by Mr Rowe of Rookwood Hall, was flattened: many hedges were ripped out, 94 acres of

22:    The first plane to land on Matching airfield: a British Lysander

23:   A U.S. bomber, based at Matching, flies over the Rodings

woodland cleared, sufficient cubic yards of concrete to cover 45 miles of roads were laid, and 350 buildings erected. Water was a problem. A water supply and a sewage system capable of supporting three to four thousand people had to be provided. Matching had no main water supply. A temporary pipe line was laid from White Roding, sufficient to maintain cooking and to provide showers.

Then an overland pipe was laid to carry water to the airfield over some distance from the famous Lily Pond, in the hollow below Matching Church. The pond was drained. Of the hundreds of water–lilies which had covered it and attracted visitors from miles around, none remained. They never have returned. At the present day it is still an attractive expanse of water, but a new pond lies on the opposite side of the narrow winding road, and the primitive machine, hidden underground, which used to pump water up to Down Hall, is obsolete and has now ceased the eerie throbbing which used to strike fear into our hearts when we were children.

Finally the mains supply line between North Weald and Harlow was tapped, trenches dug, and pipes laid four feet underground to bring water to fill a tank able to contain 50,000 gallons.

Lorry loads of bricks and building rubbish from the houses in East London and the Docks, destroyed in the Blitz, rumbled through Matching Tye and across the Green to dump their loads as hard core for new buildings and runways.

24:    Working on the airfield by hand before heavy equipment arrived

Matching and the surrounding villages were still without electricity at the end of the war, so there was no hope of linking up with a mains electricity system. Until a generator was installed, the engineers had to manage with kerosene lamps; but as soon as equipment was available, a 5000 watt generator took over with a central system for switching off, since air raids were not infrequent during 1943.

The 834th Engineer Aviation Battalion only had a few trained electricians among their engineers, and each of these had to train others while they were carrying out the installation, so that they could build up a strong maintenance team. Eventually they built their own sub-station, and a permanent line of 11,000 volts was linked to it from Bishop's Stortford power station. There was no end to their resourcefulness: they added a powerful generator powered by a diesel engine in case of emergencies and mobile generators for the Medical and Film Units.

Throughout the building the engineers had, of course, to cope with the unreliable British climate. After a spell of good weather to encourage them at the beginning of their work, incessant rain soon disillusioned them. Essex clay is notoriously sticky and heavy after rain and the mud appalled them. They called it "The Battle of Matching". Mud seriously hindered their operations and

25:    Bogged down in mud. Building Matching Airfield, 1942-3

26:    At last! A water tower at Matching

1943

27:    Hangar at Matching Air Base 1943

■ Aircrew discuss tactics as their B26 Marauder is 'bombed up' at Matching Green

28:    American airmen at Matching Green

they had to work a night shift under a terrible lighting system at that time. In addition, they not only had to construct an aerodrome, but had to be able to defend it. This entailed one day a week compulsory training; it was probably a welcome break.

With such a tight schedule it is amazing that they had time for leisure activities. But American servicemen are well-known for their generosity and liking for children, and since they were away from home for the usual celebrations, they gave entertainments and presents at parties for local children at Easter and Christmas. Each company too was encouraged to adopt a Blitz orphan from the East End; Rita, Sylvia, Sheila, and Patricia were four little girls they visited and entertained and spent their money on. Among many comedians and musicians who came to Matching to entertain them were Bob Hope and Adolphe Menjou. Matching girls were invited to dances, and Matching people invited the airmen into their homes.

The 834th Engineer Aviation Battalion officially handed over the aerodrome to the American Airforce in November 1943, and by January 1944 they had moved to Chiseldon where living conditions were apparently much improved, and they were able to train there more intensively for their final move to the continent to prepare a landing base in Normandy.

The Americans in Matching

29:   Children receive gifts from the Americans, Easter 1944

30:   Girls from surrounding villages dancing at Matching aerodrome, 1942-3

31:   Four Blitz orphans are entertained by the American Engineers

The 391st Group of bombers from the American 9th Air Force moved in, and in 1944 alone flew 6,000 bombing missions, bombarding the Dutch coast in particular. As the war increased in ferocity we were all aware of the building–up of a tremendous force around us. One hundred and ninety US airmen lost their lives from their Matching base: only a plaque in Matching Church reminds us of their sacrifice. By the end of 1944 the whole American bomber group moved on to France and the RAF took their place in Matching, using it first as a training ground, and during the onslaught of 1945 as a base for the final bombing attacks.

By the autumn it was obvious that a military manoeuvre of great importance was being planned. There were massive troop movements and intensive training at coastal resorts around the country. No enlightenment came over the wireless; secrets were well guarded. We could only guess that some tremendous plans for crossing to the mainland of Europe were afoot; when and where was pure speculation, and we were warned that "talk costs lives".

1944 was not an easy year. In June we knew what the secret manoeuvres were about. The D–Day landings on the Normandy beaches took place. We were riveted to our wireless sets and read the newspapers avidly. This was going to be the great breakthrough; the end of the war must be in sight.

But within a fortnight, Hitler launched his revenge, the diabolical flying bomb, the Doodle–Bug. To me and to most people it was much more frightening than previous bombs and landmines, although they may have done more damage. It was a question of time and sound. When a bomb had fallen, the sound of the explosion on impact with the ground was the first indication of its presence. You breathed a selfish sigh of relief that you had escaped it. Doodle–Bugs were unpiloted bombs launched like rockets from bases along the Dutch coast. They clattered noisily across the night sky at a much lower level, only just above the roofs and the tree tops, trailing a red spurt of flame behind. At a pre–set time and distance the engine cut off. We waited in uncanny silence for the bomb to dive to the ground and explode. The anxiety was unbearable. There was no crater, but widespread blast destroying large areas, and in London the damage from glass splinters in the cloud of dust and bricks was frightening.

Over 200 Doodle–Bugs were directed towards London in the first twenty–four hours: constant Alerts and All Clears went on all day and night, and anti–aircraft guns belted flack into the air, more successful with these flying–bombs than they had been with enemy aircraft. In a fortnight 2,000 people in London alone had been killed by them, and thousands more homes destroyed. London went back to living in shelters and in the Underground stations. Bombers from all around us left throughout the night to find the launching pads, but still they came. In Kent and Sussex hundreds of barrage balloons were tethered, and they proved the best antidote to Doodle–Bugs since they came over too low and mercifully got entangled and exploded.

I was tired. By the middle of July we went down to Matching for the weekend; I was to stay on for a short break with the children. Woodville was to be our haven of rest.

To our horror the very first night we were there we were awakened by the same clattering noise. We rushed to the bedroom window; there, crossing our orchard was the abomination. The engine cut off clear of the village and dropped into the countryside, causing no loss of life. It was a stray, we told ourselves; but it was unnerving.

Chapter VIII

Chapter IX

A Wartime Journey

1944 was proving to be an eventful year. We decided that however difficult it might be, we would try and go down to the West Country for a short break in August. We dare not leave it any later; our third child was due in September. This would mean a two-year gap between each of our first three children.

We were happy about the prospect of a third child, but Mother was inclined to sigh. I was heavily on the defensive and stated in no uncertain terms that I would not have the birth of any child of mine treated as a catastrophe, or even a problem. They were going to be happy children and I refused to allow her to regard this as anything but a welcome event.

"Oh well, you always said you wanted six boys," shrugged Mother. "Go on, and let's hope you can cope."

I don't think the children ever thought they were in danger in Buckhurst Hill; they could sleep through almost anything. However, with so much loss of sleep, anxieties, and demands of young children, G and I were struggling with an easily aroused irritation, and since John and Diana were at their most interesting and endearing stage, I tried to give them as much of my time and energies as possible without dissolving into tears or administering a slap if one of them fell in the flour bin when I, perhaps mistakenly, allowed them to help when I was doing the cooking. Sweeping up flour from the cracks in the rush matting on the kitchen floor was a repetitive and thankless task.

In August there was a welcome lull in Doodle-Bug attacks; the balloon barrage was working. Our troops were pressing forward in France. In July Caen had at last fallen.

Amy, a colleague of mine when I first left college, had married an architect, Roger Pring, who had had to give up his career because of serious and increasing deafness. They were struggling to build up a garage business in Dymock, Gloucestershire. They had no children but were happy to have us for a short holiday. Our spirits rose; it would be lovely to get away from the South-East and their village had had no real impact from the war.

The journey was a problem. We had no car. There were no coaches. We had to travel by train. It would have been easier to have gone up to London and used mainline termini, but with raids and such young children we felt this was out of the question. The alternative was a cross country journey and we set out with no real appreciation of how daunting this would be. Train time-tables, if they existed, were unreliable; trains were cancelled without notice, or commandeered for troop movements, and stations were blacked out after dark.

32:    Roger & Amy Pring

Matching was our launching-pad. The taxi to Bishop's Stortford station and train to Cambridge were uneventful. After a long wait we were off again to Bletchley, and there an interminable wait for a train going to Oxford. In my mind Bletchley has remained the most dreary and inhospitable place where I have ever been forced to waste time; it seemed a good thing to me when it eventually appeared to have been swamped by Milton Keynes. I'm sure this is quite unfair and circumstances exaggerated its lack of appeal.

They were steam trains, and the children were already filthy from soot, and after the initial excitement, sleepy and fidgety in turns. Finally we reached Ledbury and were picked up by Roger in his car. We relaxed; it was the first real break we had had since the war broke out. Their home, Well House, was a typical sixteenth century black and white wood-framed building, with a charming secure garden to protect the children from cars drawing up in the forecourt for petrol. Amy helped with the pumps so I took over all the cooking so that meals would be reasonably regular. By now I was well trained in adaptability and soon learned to cook on calor-gas in their large brick-floored kitchen. There was a convenient drain indented in the floor so with a bucket of water and a stiff broom

33:    Roger & Amy with me in Epping Forest

Chapter IX

the floor could quickly be sloshed down. G was in his element helping Roger with mechanical problems in the garage during the mornings, but joined me every afternoon to wander around fields and Gloucester lanes with the children. Diana needed carrying if we ventured far. It was warm and peaceful, spindleberries were in bloom in the hedges, and the war was a long way away.

In the evenings, when the children were in bed, the Octopus came into its own.

Roger's deafness was a grave handicap. Alone, Amy could communicate with him directly. Several people caused confusion, and he became isolated. G had put his mind to this before we left home and had made this Heath–Robinson contraption, resembling an octopus. He had bought lengths of gas–piping, some rubber joints and three rubber bicycle handle grips, and connected them into a four–legged object which could be put into the centre of the table with a leg each for Amy, G and me ending with a handle-grip to speak into, and with a fourth leg with a rubber end for Roger to plug into his better ear. It worked. We could all communicate. Arguments and discussions raged furiously and we put the world to rights each evening. We were all excited that Roger could hear everything and join in.

Actually he had a distinct advantage. If he disagreed profoundly with any argument, he removed the plug from his ear and launched into a fierce exposition of his point of view. No amount of waving to indicate that he should put it back into his ear so that we could join in again moved him one jot. He held forth until his argument was complete. It was infuriating; but we were glad to see his increasing isolation breaking down.

We stayed for a fortnight, busy and refreshed after the noises and stresses of the South–East of England. Down there they had seen and felt little of the war. Eggs were plentiful, although I suspect the farm which supplied them was illegally holding some back from the Egg Marketing Board to sell locally. Baskets of mushrooms arrived fresh in the mornings, picked from meadows still wet from dew. It was good to be there.

Then came the journey home. We could not have anticipated that it would be so much worse that the outward journey. We started early, but the day ground on, with once more a long wait for a connection at Bletchley, a station so dreary that there was nothing to point out to the children in an abortive attempt to keep them amused or even mildly interested.

By the time we finally reached Cambridge it was evening and the station was blacked out. There were positively no more trains that night. Since I had been in college in Cambridge and knew it well, I left the children with G and set off to find accommodation for the night. I might have known that hotels and boarding houses would eye my advanced pregnancy with deep suspicion. I had only a month to go. The Railway Hotel was full. Dozens of travellers had been forced to terminate their journeys and were already installed.

"We would sleep on the lounge floor," I boldly offered.

"Impossible. The lounge is already full," the manager replied firmly.

I scurried the length of Station Road, calling in at all possible houses. When the owners looked at me on the doorstep, out of breath, and I mentioned two small children to accommodate as well, caution over-ruled any sympathetic concern. They were not going to risk two howling kids and a possible birth even for one night. No one could or would take us in. G might have done better I decided as, thoroughly disheartened, I tramped back to the station. We would have to make the best of it there.

It was dark and cheerless, the long platform crowded with soldiers, and the waiting rooms half-full of travellers already resigned to an uncomfortable night. There was no Buffet or food of any description for the ordinary traveller; only a NAAFI for the Army. I must have looked tired and disconsolate. I certainly felt it. A young soldier disappeared into his canteen and quickly came out and thrust a mug of tea into my hand. It was a totally unexpected gesture and I was very grateful. I hope he was happily married too, and survived the war. I have never forgotten his kindness. I could cope again after that mug of tea.

A telephone was working so we rang my parents to warn them that we would not be home that night. The we rolled up clothes for pillows and mattresses and settled the children down to sleep on benches in the waiting room. They were dog-tired but singularly unperturbed and were soon fast asleep. Some men were already asleep on the floor, stretched out flat on their backs with their heads on their luggage. I, who had prided myself that I could sleep on a clothes' line, thought that was hideously unendurable under the circumstances. Eventually G and I sat down on hard chairs facing a heavy oak table in the middle of the room, and with our heads on our folded arms slept fitfully till dawn. We heard a troop train leave during the night and we had our rest punctuated by the snores of the men on the floor.

The children woke hungry and indescribably filthy and crumpled. They had smudged their faces with their sooty fingers, so we licked our handkerchiefs and rubbed, making very little impression. We then found a cold tap and washed them as best we could, and fed them on a few curled up sandwiches and battered biscuits left from the day before's packed lunch. We left for Bishop's Stortford on the first possible train, stopping at every station en route. Father had sent a taxi to meet us so we broke our journey home once more with a blissful rest at Woodville. I had always grumbled at Mother's feather beds which needed shaking from each corner every morning; I sank into them and appreciated them as never before.

Back home in Buckhurst Hill the Doodle-Bugs were absent and we read and listened avidly to news of the progress of our armies, hoping to hear they had reached German frontiers. It was not going to be as easy as that, but a new spirit of optimism was abroad.

Hitler was not crushed yet. By the beginning of September he had launched another weapon of vengeance, the V2 rocket. On September 8th the first one hit London. It was not at first recognised as a bomb. Some terrific explosion made an inordinate amount of noise and a huge crater in the ground. People even thought it might have been a burst gas main as there was no sound to signal its approach. The second fell in Epping on the other side of us and the noise and reverberation could have been anything — perhaps an explosion at the small arms factory at Waltham Abbey? There was no immediate official explanation, but as the number of explosions increased we were told that these were rockets aimed at London from the coast line in Holland and that they were travelling faster than sound. This accounted for the unexpected explosion and the prolonged noise afterwards. They were devilish; but if you heard it, it had at least missed you.

Thousands more of our troops were now leaving every day to be dropped as paratroopers in Holland or to land from gliders. Some were to attempt to sabotage launch-pads, most were joining allied forces under Montgomery pressing on towards Germany. News of appalling fighting around Arnhem reached us, sometimes reporting progress and at other times set-backs.

It was clear that our casualties were terrific, three times as many as in the Normandy landings. Another V2 fell in Leytonstone. On the 26th of September bad news arrived that we had evacuated Arnhem.

Clare was born that night, not so dramatically as Diana but in a decent civilised way, giving me time to get to the Nursing Home and allay the fears of staff that I would produce her at home or on the way. She was the prettiest of our children, and with her fair curls and shy eyes, a remarkable copy of my mother. We now had three children under four until John and Diana had their birthdays in November. "A handful," as our friends remarked.

Chapter X

The Winter of 1944

G brought the children to fetch us home. John stumped up the stairs and went straight to the cot to inspect his new sister. His smile showed his pleasure. She resembled him, and perhaps because of this, there has always been a bond of sympathy between them as they have grown up. Diana came to me, fixed me with her serious brown eyes and announced indignantly,

"Big girl HIT me!"

G hastened to explain that she had encountered a young bully on the Green outside the front gate. All was well, he assured me. I made light of it but it was obviously a burning topic for her. She settled herself on the seat beside me in the taxi, appealing in her pink coat and pink bow in her wispy hair, and reiterated firmly with a sideways look at me to see if I was properly impressed, "Big girl HIT me!". I hugged her close and forbore to demand what on earth she was doing outside the gate alone at less than two years old. It was time I came home to keep an eye on her.

Autumn slid into winter. The horse-chestnuts on the Green shed their last remaining curled brown leaves. The weather turned cold, the air was frosty and the wind had an Arctic nip. We understood that central heating was something Canadians and Americans, and even Swedes, revelled in, but the English, certainly in the country, regarded it as an unachievable luxury. We relied on three open fires downstairs and one small movable electric fire. Only the fire in the kitchen-cum-living room was kept going regularly, since it heated the "back boiler" which supplied our hot water.

Coal was strictly rationed, and as the winter became more severe, often unobtainable. It was delivered to the depots by train but coal for domestic use was not a priority. Only the presence in a house of the very young, the very old, or an invalid could be used to persuade coal merchants to part with small supplies from their meagre stocks. We managed. My father at Matching taught us how to make combustible balls by mixing mud or clay with the surplus of coal dust in our cellar, which seemed to form a large part of each ration. It was a disgustingly messy business shaping these by hand, and we had no outhouses in which to indulge in their concoction.

We collected dead wood from the forest too and propped it across the pram to support it. No wonder our beautiful white-lined pram grew yellower and shabbier; but it was perfectly adequate, with no springs broken. Our new baby, Clare, could be tucked up warm in it, and with some ingenuity Diana and

34:　G with a pramful outside 6 Hills Road: "Do mind where you put your feet!"

John could occasionally be accommodated at the opposite end, frequently admonished,

"Do mind where you put your feet!"

John at four was going to a Nursery School in the mornings. It was purpose-built in the garden of some friends from church whose daughter, Ruth Carter, was Froebel trained. All young mothers go through the trauma of leaving a clinging child to the mercies of the nursery teacher. Ruth Carter was splendid and took it quietly and calmly in her stride. John apparently settled down as soon as I left and when I returned for him at noon I had difficulty in prizing him away from his new-found toys. It was a gallop to get him there in the mornings, since the nursery was a quarter-of-an-hour's walk away, and I had to push the pram with the other two; and a real effort to return to fetch him and climb uphill all the way back.

But the short interval at home was worth it. I could at least clear up the ashes from the grate without John helping, and strewing small shovel-fulls at random on the hearth-rug. I could feed and bath the baby in peace and prepare

35:　G with the three of them on Connaught Waters at Chingford

lunch before leaving again. Without Shah our home would have been increasingly sordid. She banged cheerfully round the house, sweeping carpets, endlessly washing up and washing clothes and carrying on a jollying conversation with Diana, who fortunately was the most self-contained member of the family, amusing herself happily for hours with simple toys, colours and paper, dolls and a fragile second-hand dolls' pram. The back garden became smaller and dustier as a scooter and a series of passed-on tricycles charged up and down.

My mother's Suffolk cousin Emmie, who had looked after my sister and me with Mother when we were babies in the First World War, and whom we found vastly entertaining as we grew up, commented to me many years later when our children had all made a success of their various careers,

"Of course, all your children are clever. That's because you always talked to them so much."

I was not aware that I talked to them any more than any other mother. Just natural verbosity, I guess. But I do know that even now as a grandmother, it upsets me when young mothers ignore their small children, who are anxious to say something very important to them, and continue a long and trivial conversation with friends totally unaware of the child's urgency, brushing their tugging hands aside as a rude intrusion. They miss so much when they have no time to listen; and every day brings new revelations, new excitements, magic and skills to a child, who is anxious to share them.

Diana would converse fluently at two and could read almost anything by the time she was five. A solid, four-square figure, full of imagination and energy, she rollicked through life, mopping up words, ideas and information like blotting paper, and entertaining us with all her fun and sense of drama.

During November and December of that year, 1944, V2 rockets continued to land in the South-East, as well as an occasional Doodle-Bug. As many as a hundred fell on London then and a further seventy either fell short or over-spilled into Essex. We were very aware of them, especially when one fell in Hainault Forest on the other side of Chigwell and we felt the earth shake while the noise rumbled on. We all watched cracks developing in our bedroom ceilings, and picked up slates and tiles dislodged from the roof; but our problems were minor ones.

A new exodus was going on from London. Hundreds of houses and streets had been demolished where the V1s and V2s had struck. The cold winter found many hundred of people with no glass in their windows and gaping holes in walls and roofs from such horrific explosions. Many stayed on with makeshift doors and windows in spite of the severe weather. It was hard and they were tired. We were entering the sixth year of the war, living on hope, but sick of the dreariness of wartime England with its rationing, its blackout, its boring utility household goods, and the constant struggle to shop, feed and keep warm. Clothes were impossibly expensive; even necessities cost 150% more than in pre-war days.

We unexpectedly became the recipients of a regular parcel from America. One of the young mothers taking children to the Nursery School was Nancy Butler, the American wife of Clive Butler, a consultant at the London Hospital, who lived quite near us in Buckhurst Hill. She and I, careering up and down hills with our loaded prams, became firm friends. Her mother in the States saw that some of the parcels which she helped to despatch to England found their way to us. We were very grateful.

It was a great excitement to open these parcels. They contained all sorts of things in short supply, but chiefly clothes - for children and adults. Since I am small most of them swamped me, so I had to do much adjusting, cutting and sewing. The greatest joy to the children was the *floating soap*. Any soap was welcome, but this was special, a strange phenomenon. No amount of pushing it to the bottom of the bath would drown it. It promptly rose to the surface and floated. Neither G nor I had a satisfactory explanation for that, but it certainly made bath and bedtime more attractive.

Nights were grim from Christmas onwards into 1945. This was not so much from enemy action, but from the grinding, throbbing sound of our Lancaster bombers, heavily laden, passing overhead soon after dusk every night in steady droning succession, setting off on their terrible raids on German cities. Imagination had to be blunted: the appalling destruction and death toll was unacceptable to us if we dared to consider it. The awful devastation of London and Coventry and damage to other historic cities could not justify it; yet there seemed to be no other way now, than to see the war through to total capitulation. France had been liberated; our bombers were pounding German cities and defences. Dresden was destroyed; 2,500 bombers attacked Berlin on one night. The army of the Rhine moved steadily forward at last. We had to be grateful to those bomber crews carrying their gruesome burden on such dangerous and devastating missions. The end must soon be in sight.

Towards morning the Lancasters returned. We listened to them limping home, lightened of their bombs, many revealing their damage in the sound of their struggling engines, and many with their crews depleted. All around us RAF and USAF stations were counting them in. We tried to settle to a short stretch of uninterrupted sleep before Clare's six o'clock feed. We had given up sleeping in the cupboard under the stairs some time before and were grateful to be in our own bed upstairs. John had progressed to a bed, Diana had taken possession of the cot, and Clare could stay in the carry-cot for the time being.

A toboggan brightened my life as the weather intensified. G had knocked up a basic model, and with snow on the ground and a ten minutes' walk to the shops, it was invaluable. John had to sit at the back with the baby propped between his legs and Diana in front. I could pull them across the Green and along the pavements, negotiating kerbs with some difficulty, and we could return home with Diana hugging the shopping. If Shah was at home we could leave Clare in a pram in the garden, and with only two on the sledge, each able to hold on firmly, we could reach a cracking pace. It was not to be recommended on all occasions, but it created a pleasant diversion and made an expedition of a shopping trip. I remember the intense cold of that winter; the trees along the High Road were white with frost. It hurt your chest to move or breath quickly, and your breath rose like steam in front of you. People were sliding and skating on the ponds in Knighton Woods. There were new ponds there, where landmines had dropped earlier in the war. G took John on the ice on the pond on our Green: an exciting adventure. Unfortunately little hands playing with snow in knitted woollen gloves quickly get cold. The children cried with the pain, and the kitchen was decorated with wet gloves most of the day.

The war meant separated wives and husbands and sexual mores, particularly among the middle classes, were changing fast. Extra-marital adventures had always been accepted in the upper classes, and the working classes, certainly in the villages, quite easily embraced the odd illegitimate child. Mothers were warm and comfortable and usually accepted the situation with little fuss, understanding the ease with which their daughters "fell". But now the habit was spreading to the middle classes, notoriously narrow and pejorative, and much more easily outraged at a situation "worse than death". I remember the dire warnings in my adolescence, although Mother was highly diverted by the scandalous behaviour of the very rich, and shocked by the latest arrival in one of the cottages. It was not to be wondered at: our grandparents were Victorians and our parents Edwardian and now we, their sheltered offspring, were plunged in to the broken society resulting from a long war.

Anne, wrapped in a long mole–skin fur coat, chose this weather to arrive on a short visit. She was looking somewhat distraught. On her previous visits she had regaled me with tales of her amorous adventures and tended to convey the suggestion that G and I were rather dull to wallow in marital bliss with three children.

Now Anne was convinced she was pregnant. She threw herself on my compassion with a misplaced confidence in my knowledge and ability to work miracles. Her lover was a middle-aged Norwegian engaged in negotiations for Norwegian seamen who had fled to England. He had a wife and son in Norway from whom he had been separated for some time due to the war, so it was not a tenable situation. Would I please do something? I was totally ignorant of cures, and dismissed as inappropriate my childhood memory of overhearing my mother and the District Nurse talking in shocked low tones of the village girl who was threatening to use a "knitting needle". I swept Anne into frequent very hot baths (a difficult thing on our short coal rations), administered mugs of strong black coffee, and was mightily relieved when she announced that it was a false alarm. I dared her to throw herself on my mercy like that again.

She pocketed our clothing coupons, hugged us all close, and returned to Liverpool to wrestle good-naturedly with her hooligans and continue her illicit relationship. We settled down to a more mundane regime.

Chapter XI

A Bomb in Matching

A stray rocket or landmine fell in a remote corner of Matching. We were staying at Woodville when it happened. Father was galvanised into action; but not until the next morning! He ascertained over the telephone from one of his wardens on Matching Green that it had fallen in a field belonging to John Howard of Matching Hall, well away from any houses. It was useless to flounder about with torches in the middle of the night. Father dismissed the incident until daylight.

After breakfast he and G set off on their bicycles at a steady pace. They returned some time later, G highly amused and Father complaining indignantly about "The stupid old fool".

Apparently they discovered that the German missile had fallen and made a good crater near the middle of a very large ploughed field. They tramped over to it in their Wellington boots, soon followed by a straggle of curious locals. No sooner were they inspecting the crater than an irate voice bellowed to them in no uncertain terms to get off the land. It was the owner riding towards them on his horse, apoplectic at such a liberty being taken.

I had known John Howard and his gentle wife well as a child. He was a large man, red–faced, hardly ever seen off a horse, and well–known for his short temper. My sister, Ruth, and I found him quite amiable, but we were fascinated by the hook in a lump of wood which replaced his missing hand. Artificial limbs were not sophisticated then, and it seemed a clumsy tool to us. How could he cope with his dinner? We noticed that he always rode with the reins pulled through the hook.

G recounted with relish how John Howard rode up to my father and demanded what the hell he was doing walking across his field and ruining his crop. I guess that it was sown with spring wheat. Father was furious too. Here he was doing his duty in the war effort, and how else was he supposed to inspect and report the damage? They exchanged heated words, and Father and G refused to leave until they had finished their job, but the locals less sure of their ground dispersed rapidly. John Howard finally rode off, only slightly mollified by Father's obvious right to be there; and Father came home, cooled down and dismissed him as utterly stupid.

"There is a war on, you know!"

They were both growing old, constantly busy and on the alert, and tired of the war.

Mother was too. She was becoming crippled with rheumatoid arthritis, and Woodville made demands on her usually unquenchable energies. The village still had no electricity and it was a constant chore trimming and filling paraffin lamps. She had done it all her married life. Mains gas would never reach the village, but they now used Calor gas for cooking and had one Aladdin reading lamp, which worked by some kind of compression and had to be pumped up.

I was aware, too, that she was worried by a decision G and I took around this time. She felt we were mistaken, and maybe she was right. We gave up one room in our house to G's mother as a bed–sitting room with use of other facilities so long as she catered for herself when I was not using the kitchen. Throughout the war so far she had lived in a flat in South Woodford, but it had suffered war damage and badly needed redecorating and she seemed to be unable to make a life for herself of any quality. She was depressed and lonely and seemed unable too to cope on her rations, even with tea and sugar extra from us. We were finding it increasingly difficult to share with Rob, G's brother, in supporting her financially; and even visiting her regularly with small children was a problem. We finally decided to offer her the room and hoped she would be happier. We felt we were happy enough to stand the strain.

With hindsight, it was probably the wrong decision. At the time we felt we had no choice. The war was dragging on and no–one was living a normal family life. She was nervy and difficult and not easily lovable, and we were "doing good to her"; we should not have expected gratitude for that. A makeshift, often uneasy, relationship lasted for more than ten years, until in fact she was killed in a road accident. There was always an armed truce between the two grandmothers: G and I were buffer states.

My mother resented her coming to live with us; not for herself, but for me. Resentment, according to one school of medical thought, can be a factor in the spread of rheumatoid arthritis. It does not cause, but may exacerbate it. During the next ten years Mother gradually became completely crippled, until she was unable to walk or dress herself or even turn over in bed.

We were all beginning to feel the strain of a prolonged war and waiting for news of its end. Prisoners of war were coming in great numbers: Italians had arrived in the winter of 1943 and had been put to work on farms, many of them in the South or West; now as our armies pushed into Germany, the Germans were arriving as prisoners of war. They too were sent to do farm work and many were drafted to the North of England. Perhaps it was just as well; farmers generally found the Germans harder and tougher workers.

Stoke–by–Nayland in Suffolk was my grandparents' home where I had spent most of my summer holidays as a child. Now Tendring Hall, the Rowleys' mansion set in the park where we looked forward every year to the Flower Show

■ Crew of the 391st Bomb Group pose in front of their B26 Marauder 'Pink's Lady II' on April 11, 1944

36: American bomber crew at Matching, April 1944

and Fair, was a Prisoner of War camp full of Italians who were working on the surrounding farms.

Forty years later when G and I were holidaying in Northumberland we met German families who were revisiting farmers for whom they had worked as prisoners of war, with whom they had apparently kept in contact through those intervening years.

Matching also had prisoners of war on the farm, and many girls in the Women's Land Army. When I was a child at Woodville, Mr Frank Harding Jones was our landlord. His two beautiful daughters, Gladys and Phyllis, were Girl Guides' Captain and Lieutenant, struggling to turn a motley group of us girls into a couple of smart patrols. Now Gladys was married to Hedley Atkins, who later became President of the Royal College of Surgeons, and in addition to a house in town, they kept a country cottage in Matching, known as Taggles.

In the Twenties, this cottage had been known as Tredgett's Farm, lived in by old Mr and Mrs Benstead. It was a particularly run-down, rather sordid, but ancient farmhouse, with an inconvenient passage running straight through the middle of the house from front to back, doors always open and pigs and chickens ambling or scurrying through: a decidedly draughty and smelly arrangement. Mrs Benstead was always busy, wearing the same drab working clothes all the year through, a sun-bonnet marking the summer, and a man's cloth cap the winter.

37:    Taggles, the most desirable house in Matching

On her death Mr Jones had bought the farmhouse and now it was transformed into the loveliest and friendliest freshly-plastered house, with beams exposed and windows added. To me Taggles has always been the most desirable house in Matching. It stood out, just off Carters' Green on the way to Housham, surrounded by lawns and flowers, flanked by a large old barn. During World War II, while Hedley Atkins was overseas with the Royal Army Medical Corps, Gladys came to live there with her two young sons, and the boys attended the village school for a while.

When not at school, they loved to be in the old barn. This was used by German prisoners of war who were working on local farms as shelter during their lunch hour. They welcomed the boys' attention and encouraged their visits, so that the boys acquired quite a collection of home-made German toys.

Kingstons, the farmhouse home of John Howard's son Tom and his wife, Hilda Edwards, of the well-known family of millers in Bishop's Stortford, became a hostel for Land Army Girls. My grandparents' old farmhouse, Daltons, in Stoke-by-Nayland, also became a hostel for the Women's Land Army. Very popular these girls were too. They looked healthy and jolly in spite of doing really heavy work for very long hours. They were replacing men in essential jobs; only the strong could stand the pace. When they were taken by van to join village dances with G.I.s and local girls they were the ones who had to leave before the end; cows had to be driven up from the meadows and milked early next morning.

March 1945 saw the last of the V1s and V2s. Hitler had no more reprisals up his sleeve. News of his existence in a bunker and his relations with Eva Braun made bizarre reading in the newspapers. It was with relief that we learned of his suicide on April 30th. On May 7th Germany surrendered and on May 8th everyone in England was granted a two-day holiday to celebrate Victory in Europe, VE Day.

The lights went on, blackout came down, church bells rang out and bonfires were lit. We were a small community on the Green at Buckhurst Hill, but we lit our bonfire, joined hands to dance round it, and had our celebration. London went mad and strangers hugged each other, with dancing in the streets and all-night revelry. Londoners loved the Royal family, and the King and Queen had shown their compassion, visiting the bombed areas freely and sharing their grief during the Blitz. Now the masses took to the streets, thronged the West End, dancing up the Mall and clamouring for the Royal couple to come out onto the balcony to receive their greetings; and they reappeared every quarter of an hour for hours on end.

Buckhurst Hill was marking the end of the war with more restraint, but with no less joy and gratitude. Some streets had tea-parties or bonfires; most people just gathered with neighbours and friends. Many of their menfolk were still in the forces; many would never come home; others were prisoners of war in Japan and the war was not yet over there. We greeted VE day with profound joy and relief. We rejoiced that the children would remember very little and they had no previous life with which to compare the war years as they grew older. We bathed them and put them to bed as usual that evening and then arm in arm strolled round the pond and Green never moving our of earshot for more than a few minutes, but feeling a freedom not felt before in our married life. We began to make plans as we meandered, until it was dark and the chill air drove us in. The embers of the bonfire still had life, and across the plains and the roofs we could see the glow, not of London burning this time, but of bonfires linking up with others in celebration across the country.

An immediate plan was to spend a fortnight of G's summer holiday at the sea. The children had never seen the sea; we could build sandcastles with them.

We were not very adventurous in our choice of resort. I knew Dovercourt well since Ruth and I had spend many holidays there as children, and it had been my parents' favourite quiet annual retreat: good sands, bracing air, and a season ticket to hear the orchestra playing in the pavilion on the front each evening.

Since Dovercourt was in Essex, we hoped, too, that it would be an easy journey to reach there by train. The branch line, now axed, was still operating from Bishop's Stortford to Braintree, where we could change onto the Colchester line for Parkeston Quay and Harwich, which meandered along the south bank of the wide river Stour where it meets the sea. They would see small and large boats and train ferries leaving for the Continent.

We were more excited than the children as we set off during the first week in August, 1945. G had to cope with an inordinate amount of luggage, while I carried eight months' old Clare, an engagingly pretty baby with an endearing habit of twiddling a forehead curl with one hand and sucking the thumb on her other hand. At night she plucked the wool off her blanket instead of twiddling her curl. Somehow we had to manage a pram and two small children as well, so travelling had to be leisurely.

"Digs" had been recommended to us and we were well looked after; no one fussed if I draped wet nappies all round the bathroom or filled the line across the garden every day. In those days there were no disposable nappies and washing machines were unheard of. We packed dozensof nappies: butter–muslin inner ones and thick Turkish towelling outer ones, which had to be thoroughly washed or they were rough and made sore weals on the baby's legs.

Disappointment struck us when we set off for the beach. The lovely stretches of sand were no longer there. We knew there were still sea defences everywhere to prevent invasion and these had not yet been cleared, but we had not realised how they had ruined the beaches, collecting rubbish and pebbles where once there had been smooth sand. But we were not to be deterred. We found a good sandy patch and staked our claim, closely pressed by other young families anxious to avoid an indifferent play area. We spread our paraphernalia around us, leaving our newly–acquired second–hand Marmet low pram on the edge of the esplanade above us.

38:   Sea Defences at Dovercourt

39: I attempt to restrain Clare from destroying John & Diana's sandcastle

Armed with wooden spades and bright metal buckets, John and Diana were immediately busy making holes, G helping them to build sandcastles and dig out moats to fill up with water. Clare was at the fast–crawling stage and a full-time occupation for me. She was a menace to any carefully and lovingly built sand construction. If I took my eyes off her she made a beeline for any sandcastle in the vicinity, crawling all over it and crowing with delight if she also captured a Union Jack resplendent on top. I was constantly apologising for her to all the similar families around us who were painstakingly patting and turning out sand–filled buckets and erecting fabulous castles; or I was comforting John and Diana after she had wrecked their edifice. We all breathed a sigh of relief when she was tucked down in her pram for her morning sleep. Time to get out the flask for a cup of coffee, and some orange juice for the children.

It's a delight to watch young children discovering the sea. The sound of the waves on the shore, even if they are only whispering on a very flat safe beach, can be quite daunting at first. John and Diana spent hours walking gingerly into the water then running fast out, racing the waves; or laboriously filling buckets and staggering up the beach only to see the water disappear the moment they upturned it into the moat they had dug. G took them in to bathe and I carried a naked Clare in, wading as far as I could comfortably stand and ducking her in and out. It took her breath away, but she loved it and flayed her legs and arms about with gasps of delight. I was glad to have her with me because I'm a reluctant swimmer. There was no opportunity to learn to swim in my village or school. Clare gave me an excuse to mess about in the water without having to branch off into a neat breast stroke or attempt a smart crawl. G flung himself in like a clumsy porpoise and could swim strongly. Luckily all the children have followed his example and become strong swimmers.

THE GARDENS & QUEEN VICTORIA STATUE, DOVERCOURT BAY.

40:    Dovercourt Bay, Essex, in the 1930s

Parkeston Quay was only just down the hill from where we were staying. Suddenly one morning all hell was let loose. Every ship's siren in the docks set off a cacophony of sound, answering each other until the whole of Harwich and Dovercourt areas were drenched in the wail and All Clear sound of dozens of sirens.

It was August 14th and VJ Day. We all stopped in our tracks; the war with Japan was also over. We listened and understood, but for us the war had been over for three months now. Of course we were relieved, but it was not possible to separate the surrender of Japan from the horrific atom bombs dropped the week before on Hiroshima on August 6th and three days later on Nagasaki. A terrible evil had been released on the world, only dimly perceived then.

While we rejoiced to hear the sirens, G and I talked with horror and disbelief of the awful power of the atom bomb. What sort of a world had we brought our children into? We were told that it was necessary to bomb Hiroshima and Nagasaki to hasten the end of the war with Japan; even then our faith was uneasy at this official justification. Nothing could justify such obscenity. Now, nearly fifty years on, the danger and the guilt still haunt us.

Fortunately the children were too young for us to attempt an explanation of the noisy sirens. The sun was warm, the sea attractive and boats have a fascination for us all. We still had several days' holiday to enjoy. Our landlady was a kind, motherly soul, happy to keep watch over the children asleep in bed each evening. We never stayed away long, but at last we were able to enjoy good long walks briskly along the promenade or around the quay, simply revelling in peace.

A Bomb in Matching

Chapter XII

Aftermath of the War

Relief was our strongest emotion at the end of the war. If we had hoped for dramatic changes in our day-to-day life we were quickly disillusioned. Rationing of basic foods, including bread, continued for several more years. In country areas a system of barter was sometimes possible, though probably not legal; a dozen eggs for a bag of flour; a bag of potatoes, now also rationed, for a joint of meat. We looked at the whale meat now available in the shops and were not attracted.

I became so used to turning leftovers into yet another concocted meal, that even today I'm incapable of throwing away a chicken carcass without first boiling it up for stock, and even leftover vegetables I automatically liquidise and add to soups. In our present society where everything is expendable or can be bought ready cooked and enticingly packaged, even my family think this is overdoing it. I try to refrain from pointing a moral.

Fortunately Clare was soon onto solid foods because such bare necessities as babies' bottles and rubber teats were in short supply. I used each teat until it was so soft and the hole so stretched that the poor child was gulping the milk down at an alarming rate and burping uncomfortably afterwards.

There were a few tins of concentrated fruit or vegetable baby foods in the shops, but they were much too expensive for us. I sieved, grated and mashed small quantities of everything: spinach, carrots, cabbage, apples and plums.

I'm not gadget-minded as so many friends are: I put this down to being a new wife during the war. There were no gadgets. We saved every scrap of metal, even used razor blades, to be collected for the war effort. Electric appliances, if they existed, were quite outside our budget. I remember using my mother's large wooden-walled circular sieve for all my efforts; it fitted comfortably over a mixing bowl, and its only disadvantage was its size for washing up.

There was one apple tree in the garden, a James Grieves, whose fruit was delicious raw or stewed. It was a wonderful standby and a challenge to climb all the year round.

John had only to look at a tree to start climbing. As he grew older I had to discipline myself not to curb his adventurous spirit. I can still recall how my heart turned over when I saw him at the top of a very tall oak in Knighton Woods. My attention had been distracted by the two small girls. Almost, I shouted to him to come down at once. Instead I managed to smile bleakly and, hoping he would follow, inform him that we were moving on.

41:    In the "garden" at 6 Hills Road

One September morning in 1945 when I was organising myself to take him to school, he was playing with G's pick–axe, left out in the garden overnight. With a mighty effort he swung it towards his shoulder and promptly let it fall.

Clare chose that moment to crawl across the grass at his feet. She screamed and I rushed to pick her up. Her fair curls were matted with blood above her forehead.

John dropped the pick–axe and scrambled in panic to the top of the apple tree. He stayed there for the next hour; I forgot him. With Clare in my arms I ran the length of the High Road to where a doctor lived on the edge of the forest. He assured me that it had been a glancing blow and the damage looked worse that it was, but I must take her to the hospital for a tetanus injection.

That was ten minutes' walk away, so I ran back for the pram. G had failed to persuade John to come down from the tree, but I had no time to stay now.

The hospital visit over and Clare looking her usual smiling self, I was reassured, but so great was my trust in Dr Foster–Smith, our doctor in Woodford, that I rang him and told him what had happened, and he

42:    Clare and Diana (with handbag)

immediately offered to come and look at her. I was grateful; not that Clare showed any cause for concern when he arrived. She put on her party piece by attempting to turn somersaults on the hearth–rug. At last John was reassured. I had managed to coax him down and comfort him, but not until he saw Clare's antics could he accept that she was back to normal and join in the laughter.

Choosing his first school had been a problem. It would have been easy to send him to the church school across the Green. But John had enjoyed his Nursery School so much and as we had watched him develop under Froebel methods, we looked around for a good private school with a Froebel trained Head.

I took him to see Miss Lord in Loughton; she was Froebel trained and we liked each other on sight. I restrained myself, as I suspect all school teachers have to, from pointing out to her that my child was "sensitive" or "highly–strung". She had met my kind before. She obviously understood young children, was efficient and relaxed with them, and had a delightful sense of humour. It was the beginning of a long and happy relationship with the school. It moved that same year to Oaklands, a large, comfortable house, with spacious gardens. John could stay until he was seven and the girls would be able to stay until they had taken the eleven–plus.

Miss Lord completely won my heart when Diana started there in 1947 when she was five years old. One day she came home to lunch and refused point blank to return to school in the afternoon.

"I have to do my dolls' washing."

I phoned Miss Lord and explained the situation, and with great understanding she immediately replied,

"Of course; that's most important. Tell her to stay at home and get it done." No one fussed and the situation never arose again.

The financial strain of private education was to prove considerable. G and I were young and healthy and squashed any qualms; somehow we would earn the extra money. I joined Pearl one evening a week as an Assistant Warden at the Youth Centre. I, who am not noticeably athletic, spent most of my time rushing up and down a netball pitch umpiring a game of which I knew very little. The youths were much bigger than I was and we were often joined by hefty members of the football team anxious for exercise and an opportunity to show off their muscle power to the girls who were much more deft than they were. With a great show of energy and supreme but misplaced confidence, I managed, blowing the whistle loudly and gesticulating firmly to indicate directions. Never has netball been such an exhausting game, but we all enjoyed it enormously.

Fortunately I played the piano, so I was on slightly safer ground helping aspiring entertainers to put on a show, providing a back up for their boisterous rendering of songs like "Oh, what a beautiful morning ---". It was an evening away from small children and nappies and ironing, and miraculously I was paid for amusing myself.

We had to make our own amusement and light relief. In the aftermath of the war there was little to cheer us. We were suddenly conscious of the dreariness of our surroundings. It was not just the devastation of the streets and buildings in London, the obscene gaps and piles of rubble. The suburbs too had their gaps and destruction, but the state of decoration and repair of every house and cottage you saw in town or country depressed the spirit.

We drive round East Anglia now and marvel at white painted wooden cottages or newly plastered and pargetted houses, white or pink-washed, clustered round well-kept village greens, and neatly clipped thatched roofs nestling down like comfortable tea-cosies. Then, every house or cottage needed a coat of paint, fences needed mending, barns rebuilding. In the towns and suburbs paint was peeling, hedges were straggly, the pond on our Green was slowly suffocating with reeds and rubbish. Everyone had been absorbed in the services or the war effort. Getting back to normal was going to take a long time.

We looked at out blast-damaged roof and cracked ceilings, and were relieved when it was the turn of our road to have its war damage done. We were notified; it all had to be done at one time as part of an area campaign, and as quickly as possible. All our bedroom ceilings had to come down.

To speed up the disaster period we agreed to have all but one room tackled simultaneously. We must have been mad. All mattresses were lined up beside our bed in the large front bedroom. In the other two double rooms old sheets and disused blackout material covered the sparse furniture while the ceilings were demolished.

We all slept in this one room, odd mattresses piled on top of others, and the cot in a corner. At bedtime the children thought it great fun and treated it as an adventure playground to climb around and to practise jumping from level to level, generally creating mayhem. I was finally moved to smack bottoms; they were too excited to respond to a reasonable appeal.

In spite of closed doors, plaster penetrated everywhere, falling like a snowstorm, covering the whole house in a fine dust with pieces of rubble dribbling down the stairs. We had to think positively; it would all be over in a few days. We had not foreseen what a miserable few days they would be. We had no vacuum cleaner. With the indomitable Shah throwing out choice comments as we worked, she and I swept, washed and polished the house back to normal, reminding each other to look up and admire the beautiful new ceilings.

It was with relief that we went to visit Betty and Francis for the weekend in their new home in Banstead, Surrey. They now had three children too, corresponding in gender and ages with ours. We envied them their car and large garden, but were aware that they had had to furnish it with utility ranges. The visit was a great success; the children found space, new friends and new toys; the adults talked incessantly. On the Saturday afternoon G and I went off on our own to Kingston-on-Thames supposedly on a window-shopping spree. We ended up in a cinema.

It was showing the relief of the Belsen concentration camp by the Allies at the end of the war. The horror of that film has never left me.

These could not be human: sunken eyes in gaunt expressionless faces on sticks of bones, apparently dead until a slight movement of a head or limb gave a token of life. They crouched or lay in bundles along the drive-way leading to the entrance gates, most of them unaware that they were finally free, and unable to greet their deliverers. Most wore no shoes and were naked; some were clothed in strips of rags. They were too starved to wave; mute and emotionless. Around the camp some were already abandoned on a pile of bones; others were stumbling drunkenly in short bursts, aimlessly and perhaps unseeing in some fruitless search, falling and remaining crumpled on the ground. It was the most horrendous sight I have ever seen. We wept. We were ashamed that such depths of inhumanity could be perpetrated on fellow human beings.

Ours was the easy way; we were looking at a film. One of our young friends in Buckhurst Hill, Maurice Wells, later a Reader at London University, then just a student, was among the first groups sent in to take food and minister to the sick. To be able to do something must have been a healing process; but to be unable to stir some of these moving skeletons back to a healthy body and mind must have seared them for life.

In the late Seventies G and I were staying in Munich, and visited Dachau, another concentration camp, now kept as a memorial to its thousands of victims. People walked silently round looking at the blown-up pictures of the crowds of inmates, reading the histories, and visiting the gas chambers. It was a shocking monument to the holocaust, and to both of us it brought back the appalling impact of that film.

During the Fifties when Harold Johnson was our minister at the Congregational (now United Reformed) Church in Buckhurst Hill, he told a moving true story of those war years.

A crowd of Jews with their families had been rounded up from their homes and were being led through the streets by their German guards in a long straggling line to embark in trucks at the station for concentration camps far into Germany. The neighbours and strangers gathered along the pavement to watch them go by. One little girl among the prisoners had been separated from any relations and when she spotted a neighbour in the crowd of onlookers she waved and called out. Immediately the guards approached the woman.

"Are you her mother or a relative?"

With only a moment's hesitation she said that she was, and was promptly ordered to join the prisoners. She picked up the child in her arms and walked with the queue to her ultimate destruction.

Chapter XIII

A Visit to Sweden

Out of the blue a parcel arrived from Sweden. It was autumn, 1947; rationing was still tight, furniture boringly utilitarian, clothes and fabrics dull, limited in design, texture and colour. The parcel was a box of delight. It came from Gullan and Wilhelm Davidsson, with whom I had stayed in 1937 on an exchange visit with their daughter, Britta. It contained a royal blue woollen frock for me. I shook it out: a classic shirt–waister, with a flared skirt and, a special touch, a stiffened fabric belt of its own. I was delighted, and held it up against me – with dismay. They had forgotten how small I was. Britta was tall and blond. The frock would have fitted her perfectly; it was size 16, and I was size 12.

A note with it explained that they had guessed the size, but if it was wrong, I should return it to be changed. Of course that would have been the sensible thing to do, but this was the first new bought dress since the outbreak of the war: I was not to be persuaded to part with it for a long and possibly delayed journey. I unpicked seams, highered the waist–line, shortened the length and sleeves, and revelled in wearing it as soon as my Mother's ancient sewing machine had done its work.

The following spring Wilhelm, who was chief engineer for Stockholm Harbour, came over on business and brought Gullan with him to visit us. Somehow they wanted to make up to us for the war which, since Sweden was a neutral country, they had not experienced personally. They tried to persuade G and me to visit them in the summer for a real holiday. We were tempted, but had to refuse; we could neither afford it, nor could we abandon three energetic young children to relations and friends. They were not perturbed, and immediately said, "Bring the children too!"

Not only were they inviting all the family, but insisting on paying all return fares on Swedish–Lloyd from Tilbury to Gothenburg, as well as train fares from Gothenburg to Stockholm. It was a very generous invitation, which we gratefully accepted.

Ships have been transformed in the last fifty years. When I first went to Sweden in 1937 on the old Swedish–Lloyd's S.S. Patricia, I thought it quite sophisticated; but had nothing with which to compare it. By today's standards it was an old tub, black–painted and with very little superstructure. By 1948 it had been replaced by two new Swedish–Lloyd ships; the S.S. Britannia and the S.S. Suecia, both supposedly more modern, but looking very little different to a novice's eye. We were booked on the latter.

43:     The Davidssons, our Swedish hosts

G and I had a few qualms when we noticed the gunwhaling; how were we to prevent three youngsters climbing up and, horrific thought, toppling over? It was not to be contemplated. I found it enough anxiety to hang on to my handbag so that I didn't drop it overboard. Fortunately I had no worry about the passport because G carried a comprehensive family one.

Later, this family passport was to inflame strong feminist instincts in me: I had given up my individual passport when it was issued in 1948, only to discover the appalling sexist regulation that G could use the family passport and go abroad with it alone at any time, but I had not such facility; so, with no

44:     Britta Davidsson, in centre, wins the traditional student's cap after school finals

45:   The Swedish Lloyd *Suecia* which took us to Sweden in 1949

46:   Diana and Clare mercifully still on board the *Suecia*

other passport, I was unable to travel alone. It has taken the modern feminist movement to remove such a blatant injustice.

In 1948 it worried me not a jot. I was grateful for G to cope with passport, papers, tickets and money while I tried to keep a beady eye on the children chasing each other around the deck, but fortunately not flouting our strict instructions not to climb the gunwhaling.

Since there were five of us, we had to be split into two cabins. I had the two girls with me and a stranger in the fourth bunk, while G and John were next door with two strangers.

It was the worst crossing of the year. The crew had no doubt of this. It even fills me with horror to think about it now. The North Sea had held no terrors for me ten years before; the crossing had been cold and grey, but quite peaceful. I was not prepared for the mountainous waves and horrendous storms which raged all night as we ploughed through the sea.

We were all fast asleep when the lashing of waves on the portholes awoke us. I tried to sit up, but the ship was rolling so badly that I hastily lay down again. Then I noticed the curtains on each side of the porthole. They were behaving in an extraordinary manner. They were sticking stiffly out into the cabin at an angle of 45°. It wasn't possible! Then it dawned on me with horror that they were hanging straight down, and it was the boat rolling at such a dangerous angle. G assured me that the boat was perfectly safe with modern stabilisers, some ingenious mechanism whereby the ship would always right itself again. I had to believe him and not panic.

The girls were waking up opposite me; Diana on the top bunk and Clare underneath. She began to cry. I decided to venture across the cabin, grab her and tuck her in beside me. I had not anticipated the awful sensation of stepping out onto a rolling floor. Sickness overwhelmed me, but I rescued her and she felt safe as we curled up together. Why wasn't G there? He was a much better sailor and revelled in boats on a pitching sea.

The storm was still raging when morning light alternated with huge waves hitting the portholes. In my cabin we were all past moving, but we prayed a steward would manage to reach us with at least a glass of water. He did with difficulty, explaining that part of the way he had been forced to come on all fours.

G staggered into the cabin remarkably cheerful and obviously ready to do battle with the elements. We were a pitiful contrast, but grateful for him to wash all our faces and reassure us that we would survive. He brought John in and tucked him into Clare's empty bunk, and announced that he was going to find some breakfast and then go up on deck. The thought of breakfast paralysed us. I didn't know whether to be grateful that he was well and able to look after us, or wish that he was not so aggressively healthy and uppish. As it happened, only three of the ship's passengers managed to surface for breakfast and no one was allowed on deck because it was too dangerous. We had virtually crossed the North Sea and were approaching the Danish coast before the storm abated. We came back to life, freshened ourselves up and were all up on deck as we entered the Skagerrak.

It was a joy to catch sight of land. John was wearing his scarlet prep-school cap of which he was immensely proud. All English schoolboys wore caps in the Forties and Fifties. The Swedes protested that it was all so very English. Not even then did Swedish children wear any kind of school uniform. John fidgetted with his cap as he leant over the side and very quickly it was a red spot bobbing swiftly away in the Skagerrak. It probably saved him the ridicule of his Swedish contemporaries: a grey flannel suit was funny enough.

The sea journey was soon forgotten as we boarded the train to take us from Gothenburg to Stockholm. But this was not before G and I had gone through the humiliating business of tipping before leaving the ship. The chief steward stood at the door of the dining-room, bowing his head solemnly to each passenger in turn and holding out his hand for a tip. G gave him a pound or two which seemed adequate, and was all we could afford, but he made it quite clear that it was not enough and pointed to the three children. I was embarrassed, but G was made of tougher stuff and refused to increase the tip. We hastened through the door, grateful that we were closely followed by other passengers. We were quite ignorant then of the fact that tipping in Sweden was rigidly regulated by a strict code; every steward, taxi-driver or porter would tell you exactly what tip you should give him.

The train journey was bliss; the children settled down to enjoy it. At the end of the corridor a woman dispensed glasses of drinking water, and they were fascinated by the axe on the wall nearby, which was presumably carried so that you could cut yourself out of the train in the event of an accident. Best of all, we had lunch in the dining-car; no packet of sandwiches passed round and propped on your knees, followed by sticky fruit. This was the way to travel; the children were happy, and the waiter was set to spoil them. G and I sat back and sighed with relief. Maybe it was not such a bad idea to travel abroad with three children after all.

Even our travelling clothes were going to arrive in reasonable condition and not reduced to crumpled rags on the rack; a peg was provided for coats in each carriage. It was all very civilised, and since Swedish trains were electric, all the long windows on the corridors opened to admit fresh air without risking smutty faces or the dangers of leaning on the door to reach the only open window.

Seven hours later we reached Stockholm. As the train slowed down we could see the famous Town Hall across the water. It was magical. But it was

STOCKHOLM Stadshuset och Västerbron i kvällsbelysning   70229

47:     Stockholm: we could see the famous Town Hall across the water

evening now and we were tired. The Davidssons had a flat in Kungsgätan and
had booked us into a Boarding House nearby for Bed and Breakfast for the first
week. The children were overwhelmed; they were dazed at the spacious
marble–floored foyer and the gleaming brass lift in the centre which whisked
us off to a huge 4–bedded room. We sat on the beds and Diana burst into tears.
It was all too much; she couldn't understand the language and this bore no
resemblance to home.

However by the morning we were all ready for anything. The children
were happy and they knew that at the end of the first week they would be staying
on an island in the archipelago for a fortnight, bathing and running wild in the
pine woods. They were fascinated by Stockholm and the way you came back
constantly to the water front when you turned the corner of a busy street to see
more sailing boats, fast motor–boats and the regular white ferry paddle–boats.
They loved the gardens with the fountains playing, and made a mad rush for
one special statue cornered by four massive black stone lions, and sat astride
one each while we relaxed on a seat. We were unashamed tourists, eating
delicious ice–creams unheard–of in war–time England, riding on trams or buses
with letter–boxes on the back to take our postcards home, or taking a trip in a
water–bus under the bridges and round the harbour. Rations had no meaning
anymore; unlimited butter, cheese and tall glasses of milk, all consumed in a

fascinating variety of restaurants. One was reached by lift and overlooked the main waterways, one in a cellar near the Royal Palace, and another the famous Backa Heston, where the tables were at varied heights, some under canopies, others in pulpit-like structures, all in intimate quaintly decorated niches. Just as unfamiliar bananas held no delights for the children after the war, so the famed cream-filled pastries here held no attraction. We all preferred plain Vienerbröds and shortbreads.

The last day in Stockholm had to be spent at Skansen, then a unique living museum combined with a Zoo; now St. Fagan's, near Cardiff, has a similar museum. Examples of the old, original, Swedish farmhouses, manor houses, churches, log-cabins and merchants' houses from all parts had been re-erected in natural surroundings with people from the areas living there, wearing national costumes, plying their crafts and trades and showing visitors round. The children loved the gay costumes and jolly dances and finally saw, from the surrounding hills, a performance at an open-air theatre. Then we descended to the Exit by cable car; probably the most enjoyed two minutes of all.

The following morning we left by boat for the Davidssons' *tompt*, or summer-home, on the island of Ingarö. For two hours we travelled further out into the archipelago in the white ferry, waving to all the boats we passed and stopping at every small landing-stage to set down passengers or just to deliver

48:     G with the children off to see Stockholm from the harbour

the post. There were always children bathing there, usually naked. The children longed to join them. Sometimes we were rocking in the wake of a bigger boat, at other times struggling slowly through a narrow channel between the pine-clad slopes of two islands.

When we reached Saltsjöbaden, where my friends had lived when I had stayed with them before, we left the ferry, and a small taxiboat sped across a wide stretch of sea towards Ingarö, tossing and soaking us with spray. We docked at a small wooden landing-stage, unnoticed save for a sunburned muscular Swede with a wheelbarrow, which he loaded with our trunk and two cases and proceeded to push up a rough pebbled steep path, refusing a helping hand. After a ten minutes' climb we crossed a flat green field, and then abandoned the wheelbarrow before a long flight of steps to our *tompt*. The men dragged up the luggage between them, and we were there – on top of the world – with views of the sea over the tops of the pines and silver birches, and surrounded with more firs and pines.

As we crossed the garden, Wilhelm introduced us to the wooden cabin which was our lavatory, and to our horror, hornets had made a nest in it in their absence. A nest of wasps in intimidating, but these were monsters by comparison. The man with the wheelbarrow was entrusted with their immediate extinction. Wilhelm continued the ritual of homecoming by hoisting the bright blue and gold Swedish flag on the flagstaff prominent on the highest point of the garden. It was a usual Swedish custom, but we felt like Royalty.

We were given the smaller of two wooden bungalows on the *tompt*, containing little more than five divans round the walls, the larger bungalow housing the living quarters and kitchens. Everything was simple and modern but not primitive. The sun shone; we bathed by the landing-stage and ate out of doors, using whichever group of chairs and table happened to be in the sun when it was mealtimes. John found a pal on a neighbouring *tompt* and language proved no bar to enjoying games outdoors and getting into mischief. John shyly learned to copy the Swedish boy's manners, and by the end of his stay he was shaking hands and bowing stiffly to adults on taking his leave. The girls dropped quickly into the habit of curtseying after meals and saying "Tak for Mätan" to their hostess. At the same time they learned to have "boarding-house arms" and reach for food without asking for it to be passed.

There was only one shop on the island, a temporary one, while people were using their holiday homes. It was an enchanting walk to reach it, through pine-scented woods carpeted with wild strawberries and raspberries, or bilberries hiding damp patches where mushrooms grew. We could eat any number of fungi just as long as they were identified as edible in the coloured chart which hung in the kitchen. Without it we might have dismissed many of them as poisonous. A path left the woods at intervals and crossed rough tracks and odd strips of water–meadows. The shop was a busy meeting place, but no queuing. There was an admirable system for eliminating that, which has since been adopted in some British supermarkets. As we entered the shop we tore off a number from a pad on the wall and then sat down away from the counter. We could read, knit or chatter, so long as we kept one ear open to hear our number called.

In the evening when the children were tucked up in bed, we sat on under the trees, drinking endless cups of coffee. One night fireworks suddenly exploded above the trees. One of the families was probably holding a *kreftor* (crayfish) party since it was August. Wilhelm was uneasy. It was a dry summer and he had mentioned several times a fear of fire since the pine woods were full of kindling. He listened for a short time, then rose and picked up the phone. We heard his firm and courteous voice, but had no idea what he was saying, until he put the phone down and with a smile explained that he had told the family that he had children staying with him who would remember the Blitz in London and he would be grateful if they would not let off any more fireworks. The neighbours understood perfectly, apologised, and there was not another sound. I wonder what excuse he would have made if we had not been there!

After a fortnight's carefree existence, we were loth to leave. The children found some immediate compensation in the thrill of getting up at six o'clock to catch the ferry boat and then stopping at every landing–stage to pick up business men for Stockholm, all looking incongruous in city suits and carrying briefcases, being seen off by their scantily–clad families who had come down to collect the mail.

We had one last look at the city from a taxi and then ate lunch on the station, spotlessly clean with tubs of flowers. The children showed off their smattering of Swedish and we were soon shaking hands all round with complete strangers all anxious to try out their English on us. I went on board the ship at Gothenburg with some apprehension; no one else seemed to be bothering to search the sky for clouds. I need not have worried. The North Sea was like a mill–pond, and we waited off Southend for two hours in the fog before being allowed to sail into Tilbury.

Chapter XIV

Leaving Woodville

If it was Easter 1948, it was unexpectedly warm. The children swam in Connaught Waters, a favourite area of Epping Forest near Chingford. If it was Easter 1946, it was miserably cold; Clare fell forward out of her push–chair into Connaught Waters and was so wet that we stripped her, wrapped her in a coat and a pram blanket and hurried the family home.

I suspect that all parents pinpoint memories of dates and events by relating them to incidents in their children's growing–up. That was the summer the children had measles, whooping cough; or created some startling diversion by breaking a limb, passing an exam, or winning the high jump.

In September 1945 it was a birthday: Clare's first. I would bake a cake and she would blow out her solitary candle. We planned our rations carefully for weeks beforehand to make the birthday an event in the family.

As we were clearing up after the tea, the telephone rang. It was mother, obviously distressed. She had just had a phone call from my father, who had gone into Herts and Essex Hospital in Bishop's Stortford for a check–up. That very day he had seen the consultant who had the results of his tests and diagnosed cancer of the gullet. It was too late to operate, but they would arrange everything so that he could feed himself artificially. I could imagine Father's tone of voice, just stating the facts.

All through the summer Father had been unable to swallow solid foods easily and had looked drawn in the face for several months. He was never ill and we were inclined to dismiss it lightly and put it down to stress during the war, when he had been Billeting Officer and Air Raid Warden; when peace came he gave more time to organising a Men's Club he had set up in the village. We were persuaded that with rest he would feel better.

"How long?" he had asked the consultant. "About six months." He talked on to Mother on the phone, reasonably and laconically, brooking no interruption.

"I'm coming home now. For Heaven's sake don't make a fuss, my dear. There's nothing to be done. I can cope, and I shall have time to tidy things up."

Mother relayed his conversation over the phone to us, shocked, but doing her best "not to make a fuss". It was typical of him: everything was to be faced with a stiff upper lip; it was bad form and self–indulgent to show any self–pity, in fact to show any excessive emotion. He was handsome and amusing, kind, utterly reliable, and a very private man.

He went back to Woodville and we all worked hard to behave as if nothing abnormal was afoot, but it was impossible to dismiss the knowledge

49:   Father: it would have been bad form to have met his Maker unshaved

50:   Mother in 1946, already becoming crippled with arthritis

Chapter XIV

that time was short. He refused to be treated as an invalid. Nor would he allow Mother to be inconvenienced in any way. A tube had been inserted into his stomach, and he had to give himself warm liquid nourishment at regular intervals, day and night. It was a primitive form of treatment and the conditions in which they lived in the country were still primitive too.

They had no gas or electricity to heat milk during the night. Each evening Father quietly got on with the business of heating milk on a paraffin stove and filling a Thermos flask; and during the night he crept out of bed without disturbing Mother to administer to himself. It was an undignified operation; he would cope alone.

Mother was remarkable in her quiet acceptance, but her rheumatism became more crippling. During those six months, he tidied up his affairs, saw that all his papers were in order, all bills paid, and he contacted the Freemasons to make sure that they would come to Mother's help if she were unable to manage on the very little he could leave her. They spent Christmas with us so that they could enjoy the children, and both of them could benefit from an easier life with the flick of a switch for light and heat. He insisted on going to Loughton shopping on the bus, but had to be brought back by strangers because he had fainted on the return journey from weakness.

By the end of February he was too weak to get up. Mother had his bed brought down into the drawing room at Woodville, and for a fortnight he sat propped up, back to the window, facing a wall, quietly waiting for the end.

Aunt Lizzie arrived from Suffolk to support Mother. In any family crisis she was invaluable; trained as a nurse, she gave reassurance, silently moving around the house in her flat shoes, long skirts and inevitable all-enveloping pinafore, helping to keep the house running as normally as possible, and attending to Father.

He finally refused to keep up the feeding schedule. He could no longer do it himself, and why prolong his life? He was in increasing pain, and lay back with his eyes closed most of the time. I left the children with G and went down to see him. He opened his eyes and said with relief,

"It won't be long now."

He noticed that I was wearing a light green suit and admired it. Without thinking I said,

"Yes, I must soon have it died black."

All my clothes ended up black after two years' wear so as to make a change, and prolong their life. I had meant just that. In the circumstances I longed to recall such a stupid and tactless remark; but we let it sink into the silence. Before I left, he spoke again,

"I know you'll take care of Mother. You're good girls."

That was the last time I saw him alive.

The next day, Mother told me, he asked for his shaving things and a bowl of water. He sat up and shaved himself and died quietly that night. He was a proud and disciplined man to the last; it would have been bad form and unthinkable to have met his Maker unshaved.

Mother had him lying in an open coffin in the drawing-room for the whole of the next week. It was not unusual in those days. I found it unbearable, but Mother obviously found great comfort in it and visited him each day, assuring us that he looked more beautiful as the days passed. I suppose tensions relax and lines disappear; I was only conscious of how unnaturally cold he was.

Those who had worked with him during the war made a small uneven guard of honour at his funeral, and two strange men came forward as the coffin was lowered into the grave and threw a white glove in. We recognised it as a Masonic gesture, but its significance eluded us.

Throughout the summer G cycled down to Woodville on most weekends to try and keep the garden tidy, to saw wood for the fires and to pick and store fruit from the orchard. There were no immediate neighbours and it became imperative to find somewhere smaller, less remote and with more modern amenities, where Mother could cope on her own. My parents had lived at Woodville for over thirty years, Ruth and I were both born there and had married from there. Moving was not going to be easy, and the accumulated treasures and rubbish to sift through posed a daunting task. First we had to find her accommodation.

Mr Samuel Young came to our rescue.

Every morning and evening he cycled slowly past Woodville in all weathers from the blackboarded cottage on Matching Green, where he lived with his sister, to his imposing shops on Mulberry Green in Harlow. They were known as Young's — a large drapers adjacent to a grocers. Young's was part of my childhood; I think the grocery department was eventually sold, but Young's to me was always the draper's shop. Huge glass windows down to the ground displayed the fashions, and inside there were long mahogany counters, shelves of materials behind, and drawers of buttons, tapes, ribbons, and boxes of press-studs and hooks-and-eyes. Ruth and I found it exciting; it was a trip to cycle to Harlow with Mother to shop there and to handle all the paraphernalia of an old-fashioned draper's shop, which are so difficult to track down in towns now, and when they *are* found it's impossible to buy items singly or in small quantities. Everything is pre-measured or pre-counted and hung in plastic containers on rows of hooks, never in really convenient lengths or numbers. And where is the long yard ruler for measuring material?

We were fascinated by the arrangements for paying. All round Young's shop ran overhead tracks. The assistant took your pound note, twisted it up with the bill, grabbed a cylindrical metal container above her head, pressed it in and screwed on a lid, then pulled the cord. The cylinder whizzed along the line overhead and came to rest in a cubby-hole at the other end of the shop where a mature assistant presided over the till. She seized the container, took out the contents, did her calculations and put the bill and the change back in the cylinder. With a neat flick overhead the container was on its journey back to the counter. It was a riveting display.

Bourne and Hollingsworth in Oxford Street had a modified version of this method when I was a young woman. They had the same central money system and the same style of containers, but instead of rushing across overhead wires, these were popped into tubes in the wall behind the assistant and continued their journey out of sight. Minutes later the cylinder was back and the assistant was unscrewing the cap and handing out the change. A far cry from subsequent adding-machines and the sophisticated computerised tills of today.

Given time to clear out the ground floor stores impeding the free entrance to the stairs and the floor above, Mr Young felt he could make a very comfortable and cosy flat for Mother on the first floor of his draper's shop. We had not known of its existence and were delighted. Mother regarded it as an answer to prayer. She and Mr Young shared a deep religious faith; in fact, he had moved to live on Matching Green to be near a small Baptist chapel.

51:     Mother's flat, above (left) Young's double-fronted shop

In the intervening months G and I helped to pack up Woodville and managed to reduce the accumulations of thirty years and the furniture of a four-bedroomed house to sufficient equipment for a one-bedroomed flat. We were ruthless, and with hindsight, profligate.

No one valued Victoriana then, and G and I were no exception. We were not going to clutter our home, with its specially designed and made modern furniture, with a lot of old-fashioned bric-a-brac and junk. I am amazed now at the things we found no attraction in and sent to the sale rooms, where they made practically nothing. We had no room and no use for some good large pictures and prints which hung on the stairs in wide maple frames, some gilt-framed oils, the oval walnut inlaid dining-table and two large china dogs with blobs on their eyes, collectors' items now. All the bedroom furniture, including two brass bedsteads went too; we were not even prepared to give house to the brass standard lamp from the drawing-room. We did however keep the piano, the bent-cane rocking chair and a delicate china Rosenthal tea service; Ruth had the grandfather clock and the set of fruit plates with two bowls in the traditional dark green leaf pattern.

As the antique shops proliferate in every town we sometimes regret our ruthlessness. Mother took all that she wanted and could accommodate, taking, too, most of the huge leather or tin trunks which had accompanied them back from India after their marriage there in 1908. One domed black leather trunk, huge and shabby, contained her wedding frock and veil wrapped in layers of tissue paper; another had white cotton nightdresses and underclothes, including voluminous knickers with frills on the legs and ribbons threaded through; all of them were starched and meticulously hand tucked and stitched by my grandmother. They would never be worn again, except as dressing up clothes; but Mother must have found that link to her past too strong to break, and we made no attempt to persuade her to abandon them. By the time she had filled the other trunks with household goods the store rooms under the flat were going to be as full as they once had been. G and I found them there with their same contents when four years later we had to pack up the flat.

Chapter XV

Back to Suffolk

As chill spring days gave way to milder weather, Woodville was hard to leave for good. Round every tree in the orchard Father had planted bulbs which had multiplied until now a profusion of gay tulips jostled daffodils and narcissi for space. Plum blossom sprinkled the grass with confetti, and tight pink and white blooms struggled to open on the apple trees: Mother's favourite Ribston Pippins, Aunt Alice's rosy nameless apple, all the Codlings, Russets, and the Blenheim Oranges we stored in newspaper on the spare bedroom floor for Christmas and the winter months.

We must plan a holiday and take Mother with us to take her mind off the move. It would have to be as cheap as possible we decided, after G and I had spent an evening on High Finance.

He returned from school one day and announced that he had solved the problem. The woodwork master, an elderly craftsman who had fought in World War I, had a daughter who owned a cottage at Jaywick. We could have it for a week at a nominal rent. We knew Jaywick only by reputation: a holiday bungalow town on a bleak stretch of Essex coast near St. Osyth's with no luxuries and a minimum of amenities, but with ideal sands for family holidays. The children were too young to demand more and we were content to relax.

Mother provided an unexpected luxury, and ordered a taxi to transport us there and back. Mr Wright from Harlow would drive us.

When Ruth and I were small children Mr Wright had owned a hansom cab and two black horses. That was more than a quarter of a century before. We had anticipated its arrival at Woodville gates with delicious excitement, almost bursting with pride as we set off for Harlow station at the beginning of every summer holiday, which we would spend with our Fletcher grandparents at Stoke-by-Nayland in Suffolk. The same Mr Wright had moved with the times; he had changed his top hat for a peaked cap, and the swinging lightly-sprung cab for a limousine, which had been familiar to me over the last ten years.

On Sunday evenings from 1933 to 1939 it had taken me from Woodville to catch the Green Line coach at Harlow Post Office back to Chingford; it had driven Ruth and me to our weddings at Matching Church; it had attended all family funerals. Mr Wright was also the undertaker. In fact years earlier my parents had passed my Grandfather Salmon's plush top hat, which had to be smoothed with a circular motion before each use, and its accompanying leather hat box, along with his black frock coat to Mr Wright for the use of one of his bearers at funerals.

52:    On Jaywick Sands, August 1947

53:    The basic bungalow at Jaywick

Now Mother, three small children and G and I, were packed into it with a totally unnecessary pile of luggage, since I am completely unable to this day to go on holiday in England without preparing for all eventualities and taking clothes for every possible change in the weather. Add to this a few games and favourite toys and we were ridiculously overburdened. It was the car from door to door which really did it — "Let's take it; it's sure to come in useful."

Jaywick we found to be totally anonymous as a village; but the bungalow was reasonably comfortable and basically equipped. The children slept in bunks, and the novelty lasted the holiday. With difficulty my Mother could walk slowly and painfully along the path on top of the grassy sea-wall as far as the beach. Luckily G and I had taken a quantity of books to read. The only paper shop owner was not taking any chances on having leftovers on his hands, and sold only popular dailies, comics, and the cheaper women's magazines. In those days, when Kingsley Martin was editor, we liked to read *The New Statesman*, and enjoyed attempting the competitions; but we should have known better than to ask for it there.

The weather was so hot and the sea so warm that, in spite of sand flies on some of the beaches, we tanned a pleasant brown and ignored any housework until the last day. There was one disturbing incident. One day we watched a policeman knock on the door of a nearby bungalow and speak to the residents, but we had no inkling of his mission. A boy of eleven had drowned. The tragedy might have engulfed the whole community but, so insulated and isolated was each family in its bungalow, that we were only aware of what had happened after the family had quietly packed and gone home. We were amazed at the stoicism with which they faced such devastating news.

For parents, the great advantage of having children close together is to be able to pass larger toys down the line before they fall to pieces. Two well-worn tricycles lasted for several years, slowly disintegrating after destroying much of what was left of our steadily balding lawn. The war was over; we must tackle the garden properly.

As Christmas drew near in 1948 we decided to buy John and Diana bicycles; this entailed a trip to Gamages in Holborn, London, then a store for every practical need, but no longer there. It was to be a secret, so we had them delivered to Mrs Williamson, who fortunately had a much larger house on the corner of the Green opposite to us.

The bicycles were a great success: Father Christmas had done his research well. Unfortunately neither of the children had ever ridden a two-wheeler, and G and I were not very interested in adding stabilisers, or incurring further expense. We knew there would be a price to pay for this decision. Every spare minute during the Christmas holiday, G and I were clinging onto the saddles, propping them up and running fast beside them round the Green. It was bitterly cold, so we kept warm; but it was exhausting and time-consuming. However each of them learned to ride without too many tumbles and tears, and Clare was quite happy to career behind on the rattling tricycle on which she could just reach the pedals.

Days were short and we had to be settled round the fire after tea to listen to Children's Hour. Toy Town with Norman Shelley as Larry the Lamb was an early favourite. G and I had read all the Winnie the Pooh and Little Grey Rabbit books to them, and later progressed to Richard Crompton's *William* and *Jennings at School*. Clare was still loving fairy stories, and her special demand was for Cinderella. Every time I came to the part where one of the Ugly Sisters interjects, "I do declare!", without fail, Clare would correct me firmly, "*Not* I do declare – Clare!"

The following summer, holidays in Suffolk began again. Transport had been impossible while the girls were still babies. Now we wanted the children to enjoy the soft Suffolk countryside and the leisurely pace of life as much as we had done. We shut our eyes to the daunting travel prospects.

Every summer in the Twenties Mother had left Father at Woodville to look after the chickens and potter in the garden while she took Ruth and me to stay with her parents, Robert and Emily Fletcher, who had been tenant farmers in Stoke–by–Nayland but had then retired to a cottage there. Actually Father was avoiding his in–laws; Grandma Fletcher was far too interested in his soul, and he had no intention of allowing her to pry into his relationship with God.

54:   Phil and Emmie when they first moved into the Laurels

Souls were a compulsive pursuit of hers; she was not deterred by his sense of the fitness of things, and he thought her Very Bad Form.

For us it had been an eagerly anticipated ritual. However, all Mother's relations were dead except her red-headed second cousin, Emmie Welham, now married to Philip Pearl, a farmer from Barn Hall in Colchester. They were running a milk business from The Laurels, Emmie's old home in Scotland Street. As children, Ruth and I had found Emmie, who was ten years older than us, enormous fun, wickedly naughty, but full of laughter and plans. We were busy with her all day long. Now she and Phil had three brilliantly red-headed high-spirited children, a boy and two girls, very near the ages of our three.

We set off from Bishop's Stortford on a cross-country train to Braintree and changed for Colchester where we clambered out at North Station and fortunately had only a short way to go to the pub on the corner to pick up Norfolk's bus to Stoke.

Everyone's clothes were packed in one trunk since it was easier to park it in the luggage van and concentrate on the children. On the double-decker country bus it was accommodated with the ticket collector at the rear. We completely forgot it. Drivers changed over at the bus depôt in Nayland and some efficient worker there took the trunk off too, mistaking it for unaccompanied luggage transported from the station with other parcels as a routine job. We only

55:   Weavers' Cottages in Back Street, Stoke-by-Nayland

56: Stoke-by-Nayland, Suffolk, with the Vicarage on the left and the Village Hall in the middle

discovered the loss when we reached our terminus at the top of Stoke hill, outside the Angel Inn guarding the crossroads. G returned to Nayland on the bus to retrieve the trunk, while the children and I skipped down Scotland Street to The Laurels, the first house on the left at right–angles to the road.

I loved the old house with its worn uneven brick path, small–paned windows and cream–washed walls. It had an acre of ground, stables and sheds, and a chapel at the end of the garden. Emmie had lived there with her parents. Her father eked out a living on his smallholding, and her mother, who was deaf, cooked superbly, but her narrow religious faith drove her rebellious daughter to distraction.

The centre of her mother's life had been her large walk–in larder. By my standards Emmie was an outstanding cook too, but she had no time to spend making rows of preserves, and apple moulds to stud with blanched almonds for puddings, or bottling pounds of fruit to fill the shelves. She helped Phil with the milk business; so the larder was swallowed up in the larger living room, a transformation achieved simply by removing one wall.

I wandered round marking the changes. Cupboards and a refrigerator had replaced the larder; electricity, the candles and paraffin lamps; and a new large kitchen and dairies had been added. Outside, the old privy behind the evergreen bushes with its friendly arrangement of three seats in a row, each of diminishing size, had disappeared; modern plumbing had come indoors. The old stables still sheltered a deep well which terrified Ruth and me as children, but tools and machinery, albeit rather higgledy-piggledy, proclaimed it a workshop; and the dilapidated shed, looking a little less drunken, housed the milk van.

The children scurried everywhere, pushing through every door and peering into corners. How disappointing modern open-plan houses must be to children: no hiding-places, no secret retreats, no stimulus to the imagination. There were paths winding round the edge of the garden and a high grassy bank all down one side, with the washing line exposed to all the winds on top, and beyond it arable fields, bleached with corn in the summer. All Frank Welham's greenhouses were still there, the paint shabby and the shelves neglected, but nurturing some tomatoes, and heavily scented with sweet pea and tobacco plants; but no longer the dozens of boxes of cuttings, or rows of exotic house plants.

Apples and plums grew on old bent and lichen-covered trees planted haphazardly around the garden. It was always obvious when John had consumed too many plums, because he came out in a tell-tale rash. Vegetables and soft fruit still covered half the land, more than enough to satisfy family needs and leaving room for roses and a lawn too. Emmie's father would never have countenanced the lawn; in the Twenties every square yard had to be productive, and in any case shears were wearisome and lawn-mowers rare and expensive.

Emmie was now a plump, middle-aged version of her passionate, outrageous youth. She was still as noisily voluble and entertaining, clasping us all to her ample bosom with open-hearted generosity, accepting my help somewhat unwillingly, proclaiming with mock indignation,

"I can manage quite well, thank-you. Don't you be bossy, Mrs Collecott!"

We were rude to each other in a way that only people who are really close, dare to be.

Her kitchen, cosy with a Rayburn for cooking, was the centre of our life there. The ten of us could cluster round the large scrubbed table for meals. Emmie produced a delicious blown-up batter pudding for dinner, serving it with gravy before the main meat meal. This custom still pertains in some country districts, but the children had never met it before. I suspect it started as a way of filling hungry stomachs so that there was a subsequent saving on the quantity of meat to follow. The children were even more intrigued to be served sausages with gravy for breakfast.

Phil riveted their attention by drinking out of his saucer when he was in a hurry, and by carving joints away from his body. It looked awkward, but it was a speedy and skilful operation, and since he insisted on using a menacingly sharp knife, it was a distinctly safer method. G tried to copy him, and failed dismally.

Emmie planned picnics and outings with the same verve and ingenuity as she had always done. For picnics she would bone and stuff a chicken with the greatest of ease and swear that it was no more trouble than cutting sandwiches. Norfolk's Bus Company ran day outings to Clacton, Frinton, Walton–on–the–Naze and Dovercourt. We must all go. It made not a jot of difference that she and Phil were up at five o'clock every morning to greet the lorries which arrived with milk in churns collected from a vast area. The milk all had to be bottled in the dairies at The Laurels and then delivered by van to the doorsteps of houses in a wide country district, often demanding long detours down rough country lanes for just one customer. They were untiring. They were back for breakfast as we were getting up, and soon ready to start the lengthy business of washing and sterilising the bottles. No sooner was that over than Emmie was ready to join our expedition to the sea. Phil preferred to catch up on sleep and then spend time in his workshop or, reluctantly, in the garden.

At the end of the garden was a brick–built chapel. In my Grandmother's time it had been subsidiary to the chapel at Nayland, but it was now closed, presumably for lack of a faithful congregation and the funds to support a

57: A day out at Walton-on-the-Naze

58:     The Laurels, Stoke-by-Nayland

59:     The converted chapel on Scotland Street

preacher. The Welhams' peach tree still climbed over the sunny, south-facing wall. Apparently Emmie owned the chapel, and a few years later she had it converted into a four-bedroomed house, losing part of their acre as a garden for it. When we returned the next year for our usual summer holiday, they had transferred all their furniture and effects there, while The Laurels had had a second face-lift and further modernisation. The chapel made a modern and comfortable house and it was an interesting experience to view the garden and outbuildings from the opposite angle.

Next year we were back in The Laurels and the chapel had been sold as a desirable residence. For the first time in their lives Emmie and Phil could afford a few simple luxuries and relax their perpetual struggle. Later they were able to build another house and a bungalow on their land, so that, as they grew older, the garden became more manageable.

After a year or two, six children were a noisy, bouncing, crowd, so I sometimes relieved the confusion by setting them competitions. I don't think they resented an occasional bout of organisation; and it gave us a minor breathing-space and preserved our sanity. They were enthusiastic competitors. I sent them off on Treasure Hunts, judged selections of seashore finds after a day at Clacton or Walton, often arranged with amazing ingenuity and skill, or handed out dinner plates on which they constructed miniature gardens from materials in the garden or from the wild. Prizes were sweets for everyone, with perhaps a few more in a bag for the winner which could be shared.

Year after year we were welcomed to Stoke, the children as they grew older delighted to help on the milk-round. While she was still small, Diana was given the task of copying out the copper-plate lists of customers on the milk-round, and when John was on the round, he was so fast with the delivery of bottles that everyone sat down to breakfast much earlier.

Phil was an enthusiastic bell-ringer and drove off in his van one night a week to the next village of Polstead for a practice. At Christmas time he joined the hand-bell team which toured the village and outlying cottages in the evenings, always ending up at The Laurels where they were assured of a hot supper cooked by Emmie.

Sometimes Phil would bring out his violin in the evenings and I would accompany him on the piano. I remember that when Ruth and I were children and Emmie first knew Phil, he and his brother John both played violins in a four-piece dance band which performed in the surrounding villages on Saturday nights. Now his favourite piece was Handel's "Largo"; just as Emmie, when she played the violin as a young woman, insisted on me accompanying her performance of "Il Traumerei". If the children were still up, we played and sang hymns.

The old Ancient and Modern tune book, which Mother had passed on to me, looked very different from any later edition. Where possible, it shunned crotchets and frivolous-looking quavers and used solemn-looking minims and semibreves. As a child I thought these white open notes, sometimes even including breves, meant that hymns should be played at a funereal pace, and when later editions wrote the same tunes in crotchets and quavers, I found myself automatically playing them much faster. This probably also explained why I so much preferred playing rollicking Moody and Sankey tunes at the chapel service.

When Phil and Emmie came to Buckhurst Hill to visit us once, Diana, who was just learning, played a simple tune on her violin. Phil was interested and anxious to help; before we knew what was happening, he had found my old Ancient and Modern tune book and was pointing out to her these open round notes and encouraging her to use her bow to get a full sound from each note.

Chapter XVI

Françoise, and a French Journey

It was Françoise who started it all. In those post-war years she was the first of a long line of French students, whom we had met through a variety of contacts. All of them have remained friends over these forty years, our children, and more recently our grandchildren, exchanging visits.

Françoise came to Buckhurst Hill immediately after the war as an *au pair* to a friend of ours. I had never been to France but read and wrote French quite fluently, having followed an A-level in French with a Diploma at College. I looked for opportunities to speak it and hear it spoken. Since the town offered little or no recreation, and there was no local cinema, Françoise often spent the evening with us. Our children were in bed by half-past six. She had suffered much more stringent rationing in Paris than we had, so was quite happy to share my concocted soups and suppers.

With some dried milk, dried eggs, flour and water, I could make a reasonable batter; and with a spoonful or two of minced meat or bacon and a good sprinkling of herbs mixed in, I could fry passably tasty pancakes in some run-down fat, and at least produce a dish of savouries to eat with G's home-grown vegetables. G washed up if he were in, while Françoise and I talked in French, lapsing in to Franglais at times. She was heavily into Existentialism; we had just discovered James Joyce, so we laughed and talked until it was time for her to stroll back across the Green.

She gave us back our youth with her slim figure and lively Provençale looks. She could wear the dullest, plainest clothes - a black skirt and a dark brown blouse - with style, and look stunning. G and I decided that it wasn't so much the clothes they wore, as the flair and confidence with which they wore them, that made the French so fashionable and attractive. I envied her, as I did all the French girls who came and stayed with us; I never seemed to achieve the same results with my limited wardrobe. We are still great friends. Her mother, Madame Plasse, now in her late eighties, still reigns supreme in Paris and at their summer home in Forcalquier, Provence. My children and grandchildren don't miss an opportunity to call on her, while Françoise's sons are an extension of my family. I am never surprised to see one of them comfortably settled at the breakfast table, having crossed over from the Hague, where they now live, in the ferry, and driven up from Harwich in the early morning.

As our children grew to be teenagers, Françoise's younger sisters, Geneviève and Claude, spent many holidays with us and our children returned to France with them. When she was fifteen, Diana won an essay prize for her

60:    Françoise, "who gave us back our youth", with her eldest son

account of a journey from Provence back to Paris with the Plasses. I had not read it until I saw it in her school magazine at Loughton High School. It vividly recalls the fun these Anglo-French relations brought to our family.

A Journey

> M. Plasse had given us his instructions. He knew well that the train would be packed with home–going holiday–makers like ourselves, so that boarding it would be a matter of every man for himself. Long before its shrill whistle could be heard down the curving track he had placed us at our stations, and now, like beasts crouched for attack, we held our breath and prepared to lunge forward the second the door should swing open. 'Claude, hang on to Jérôme and the grey hold–all. Geneviève, take care of the food–basket and all your personal effects ––––'. Even Madame la Grand'mère was charged with her own luggage.

> But the organiser of these manoeuvres was typically unburdened, and stood, his ample paunch protruding from his loose trench coat, puffing at a cigarette. Then 'Suivez–moi!' he bawled with the fervour of a Napoleonic general charging into battle. We hurtled after him, our loads bumping at our sides, through the trickle of passengers descending at Avignon. But this meagre band did not deter us. It was the throng which had been waiting on the platform with us, and the multitude

awaiting us in the train, who formed the hostile force. It seemed as if the driver of the train and the entire station staff had allied with them to prevent us from making this journey, for as Michel hurled the last case through the open door and shouted 'Bon Voyage!' the engine, which had been panting in the station for less that three minutes, released its brakes and roared off down the line.

A few minutes later we had sufficiently recovered to look around us and take stock of our position. That is, to look around us as far as our crushed state of preservation would allow. We were hemmed in on all sides, not only by our hastily deposited luggage but by the hundreds of travellers who shared our fate. Monsieur resumed his dictatorial role. First the luggage was stacked into a formidable barricade. Then Claude and I were sent off in opposite directions to reconnoitre, elbowing our way through the sunburnt crowds returning from the Riviera.

The little air-space in the corridor had long been replaced by the strong-smelling fumes of French cigarettes. In the crowded compartments, tightly-packed passengers were struggling to eat oranges, read glossy magazines or do their hair. The gabble of their chatter was challenged by the continuous clink and clatter of empty 'Pschitt' bottles which, buffeted by the restless feet of standing passengers, spun from side to side, spilling their abandoned contents among the scrabble of lost labels, chewed drinking straws, and scrappy magazine covers strewn on the corridor floor.

Our search for seats was completely fruitless. 'Tant pis', was Monsieur's optimistic comment on our apologetic report. He lit another cigarette and resumed his resigned stance as he produced 'Le Figaro' from his raincoat pocket and immersed himself in the Algerian problem, occasionally muttering incomprehensible phrases into his double chin or greying moustache. Having deposited his wife and mother-in-law on two folding seats at the other end of the carriage, he felt himself no longer responsible for the welfare of his women-folk.

Geneviève was comfortably established on an abandoned ruck-sack in the corner, where, oblivious of the multitudes constantly pushing past her to the bar, she sat cross-legged with a well-thumbed paperback in her lap, smoking a rather buffeted cigarette. Jérôme was in his element now that Madame la Grand'mère was safely disposed of. He perched happily on the top of that rickety mountain of cases, prevented from falling by the pressing crowds which surrounded its foothills, and read out snatches of his Mickey Mouse comic to us in a shrill, lisping *voice. Claude and I found it impossible to do anything but stand, arms pinioned to our sides in the sweltering press ...*

Once into her stride, like all children who have found the joy of language, Diana leaves nothing unsaid, nothing undescribed, and writes vividly of the entire journey until the last phase .... She ends –

We were by now resigned to standing for the entire seven-hour journey to Paris, for at Lyons the train had only absorbed, not deposited, passengers. However Dijon was our only hope. Monsieur had already prepared for the stop. Again we were issued with our orders. As the rhythmic revolution of the pounding wheels softened down to a rallentando, he made his way down the carriage, fighting against the descending passengers. Claude and I followed, clutching old bundles, leaving little Jérôme to protect the women-folk and our luggage. Eventually, after an exhausting struggle through three packed compartments, we triumphed over the influx of Dijonnais by occupying a compartment which a family of five infants under eight years old were leaving with much commotion. Monsieur filled the doorway to ward off possible invaders, while Claude and I returned to our original stronghold to collect the remainder of his retinue.

A quarter of an hour later, when the train was well on its way again, we were triumphantly established in a self-contained apartment of our very own. Now, although the failing light took with it all prospects of a view, we settled down to the last lap of our journey in comfort as the blue train streaked through the darkness to Paris.

Claude, with her blonde hair and Bourbon nose, came on several Devon holidays with us in the fifties. Since she was always self-contained and calm, it was difficult to know if she was really enjoying herself. Geneviève came year after year in her vacations when she was a medical student. Competition was so keen for the use of the laboratories in the Sorbonne that she often broke her holiday for a few days just to make sure that she did not lose the time she had booked. She is now a dermatologist, married to an eye-specialist and her three children correspond in age to my grandchildren. The small Jérôme of the story is the son of Françoise's eldest sister, Anne-Marie; he is the same age as my younger son, and has exchanged with him years ago, when I was energetic enough to take them to museums and galleries in London and search for military insignia which was his craze at the time. He is now a writer and film-critic in Paris.

61:    Claude, "with her blonde hair and Bourbon nose"

Monsieur Plasse's mother-in-law was a formidable grandmother in her time. She ran the apartment in Paris and guarded the well-being of the souls of those in her charge. Without fail a postcard would arrive before every saint's day to remind whichever grandchild was staying with us not to miss going to Mass on that day. G and I groaned. If we were in the country it was well-nigh impossible to get her there in the morning, and in the wilds of Devon we went to inordinate lengths to fulfil *Madame la Grand'mère's* commands. We might have found it less of a chore if the French girls had shown any enthusiasm for attending the Mass and were not indifferent to it, merely wanting to carry out la Grand'mère's strictures in case she asked them if they had been faithful.

Chapter XVII
Church: A Time to Take Stock

The war absorbed G and me for the first years of our marriage. We had made no commitment to any church as regular attenders, but with small children we looked around for a church to join which would attract us as a family.

As a student in Cambridge in the Thirties I had thrown off the religious shackles of a tight village community and avoided church groups, and invitations to Sunday afternoon tea-parties by local church members; a considerable sacrifice really, because most students found this a useful way to get to know some of the "five thousand" undergraduates our Principal had warned us of during our first week up. I preferred to be anonymous at services in St. John's or King's College chapels.

Ruth and I grew up attending three services every Sunday at Matching, and at our first school we had been scornfully labelled "Devil-Dodgers" because we attended both church and chapel: church in the mornings with Father; chapel in the evenings with Mother. This division was not entirely governed by religious convictions, but by geographical distances; it was a long walk to church, usually across several fields and only suitable for a morning expedition, but the chapel was only just across the Tye and easily accessible on the darkest evening in winter.

"Chapel" had working-class connotations when I was a country girl. Village chapels usually attracted simpler folk; the parish church the upper classes, the Establishment. This was particularly true in Suffolk where my grandparents lived. The villages were more feudal and the farming community mostly tenant farmers. In Essex this distinction was not so marked. Farming was more prosperous, certainly round Matching where most farmhouses were substantial, of ancient origin, and named "halls". Housham Hall was mentioned in Domesday Book as the manor of Oversham. The owners of such farms were well-to-do farmers, many from Cornwall or Scotland, with strong non-conformist traditions. Three generations later their names are still well-known in the county: the Broads, Sopers, Andersons, Scantleburys and Tinneys. When I was a child their families added glamour to the chapel, and the wives produced a wealth of good things to eat on special occasions.

G and I had both been baptised into the Anglican church, but his family had been Unitarians. This was a closed book to me; I thought it was a Northern phenomenon. The Congregational Church was the most common non-conformist church in East Anglia. Our little chapel in Matching had been in some way attached to the Congregational Church on Hatfield Heath, and Mother took me by surprise when she told me she was a deacon; but this seemed to require nothing more than helping the Pastor's wife to run weekly Mothers' Meetings.

In the suburbs, including Buckhurst Hill where G and I were living, the word chapel was no longer used. We gravitated towards a thriving Congregational Church. We had tried the Anglican church, but found the Rector elderly and dogmatic; we thought he would quickly dismiss us as heretics. Buckhurst Hill Congregational Church was unusual. Its builders had competed with, or copied, the Anglican Church, St. John's, on the High Road, by erecting a large grey–stoned neo–Gothic building complete with a typical square tower, which made it indistinguishable from the parish church from the exterior. It would be interesting to know what inspired this similarity. Most Congregational churches of this period in comparable towns are remarkable for their dauntingly ugly buildings

We were glad to join this church. It had a large membership of professional people, articulate, energetic, questioning and caring, who greatly enriched our lives. Previous ministers had been distinguished.

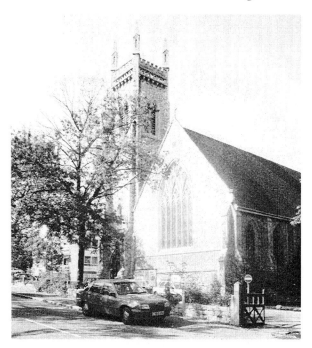

62:    Buckhurst Hill Congregational Church in Palmerston Road

Edward Shillito, whose wife was still alive and a member, had been a scholar and hymn-writer. His Easter hymn, "*Away with gloom, away with doubt*" is still included in the New Standard Hymns Ancient and Modern. He had been followed by young John Murray, who left for Emmanuel Congregational Church at Cambridge. That was considered a prestigious ministry, and had been held by Sidney Carter, who was very well-known there when I was a student. Sydney Carter's sister and several members of his family still lived in Buckhurst Hill and were members of the church. Ruth Carter, his niece, ran the Froebel Nursery School which our children attended.

A disturbing period in the church followed while we were still dithering about becoming members after John was born. Norman Perry became minister. We liked him and his warm and capable wife, who patently adored him. He was dark, handsome, tall and energetic, with considerable organisational skills; she was a much more simply committed Christian, short and lame, clever and creative with crafts. An oddly matched but loving couple, we all thought, until we were suddenly and devastatingly disillusioned. Norman joined the Congregational Youth Office in London, where he fell in love with a young and attractive secretary. Very soon he had renounced his ministry, left his wife and child, and sailed for Australia with his new love. The church community was badly shaken.

G and I were on the periphery of their lives, so knew nothing of the agonies and heart-searchings which must have preceded the move: we only saw the heartbreak of those left unceremoniously behind. War had taught us how fragile life was; but this showed us how fragile, and how overwhelming, love was. It disturbed us greatly, and we found it difficult to accept; if we were honest, we knew that we were swayed in our feelings by the somewhat sentimental belief that he was more to be condemned because the wife he had left was lame. Certainly she was desperately hurt, but his decision to leave must also have been agonising because of the handicap. As a whole the church community forbore to judge, and were impressive in their care and support. It must have been with some relief that they welcomed Harold Johnson as minister. G and I joined the church, and were lucky to have him for most of our life there. He and his wife, Una, were the same age as us, also with small children and we had much in common in addition to swapping children's clothes: the usual lack of money, a blessed sense of humour, and idealistic notions of making a better and more caring world after the hideous inhumanities of war.

Harold was tall and prematurely bald with a true tenor voice which would soar above the hymns in a fine descant. At social functions he could sometimes be persuaded to sing a solo: I recall with pleasure his jaunty rendering of, "*Oh, I like to be a ploughboy, who whistles o'er the lea*"; the haunting melody of, "*Where have all the flowers gone?*" and on Christmas Eve his clear voice

63:    Harold Johnston baptising my Nigerian god-child

from the back of the church just before midnight piercing the darkness with "*O Come, O Come Emmanuel*", gradually gaining strength as he moved slowly towards the altar, singing as he walked until the congregation finally joined in.

Not everyone found Harold's style of thinking aloud in his sermons to their taste. Certainly my mind wandered off when he pondered too long, and I imagined a class of children in school who would be restless by this time, flicking pellets across the room with deadly accuracy. Some of his congregation were used to short rounded expositions with a brisk message to "take home". Harold was not going to let us off so lightly. He was often out on a limb, disturbing, and struggling in his sermons to arouse his comparatively affluent congregation from what he saw as their complacent attitudes. For him, Christianity was not meant to be a comfortable religion, nor was it an insurance policy for the future; he constantly reminded us that God was not an optional extra. He taught us to be open to one another in a caring community, reminding us how love made us vulnerable, and that "to take up the cross and follow Him" meant the acceptance of a possible crucifixion. He thrashed himself as much as he thrashed us. G and I had a great affection for him and his family. That did not prevent me from telling him in utter exasperation one day that according to him we none of us had a chance unless we were prostitutes or sinners. He laughed with us.

Several families in the church would have been remarkable in any congregation; the Linders among them. They were a well–known philanthropic and gifted family, who owned a large house and garden which they made available for parties, fêtes and swimming galas. Mrs Linder was elderly and withdrawn from social life, so she was rarely seen; but Mr Linder was a byword for eccentricity. He was a rich old man, owner of Coubro and Scrutton, ships' chandlers, very lame, and totally unconcerned with his personal appearance. He came to church with black shoes, no socks, a shabby greenish–black suit, the jacket soiled from spilt meals, and a silver-topped ebony walking-stick. His daughter, Enid, accompanied him on trips abroad, and it was said that on these trips his appearance, still minus socks, was so unusual, that customs' officials at the airport often gave him an exhaustive inspection down to unscrewing the top of his walking-stick, convinced that he was no normal citizen and must be engaged on some smuggling racket.

He made slow progress down the church aisle, staring unsmilingly ahead, not easily engaged in conversation. Yet when his garden was open for a church occasion, he was on the tennis court, playing doubles in his black trousers and braces, racquet in one hand, stick in the other, hitting the ball with some accuracy when it approached him, leaving his partner to do all the running about. He liked to win. It was understandable that as he grew older we decided he was becoming senile. Nothing was further from the truth. His witty speeches when he publicly welcomed us all to his garden, delivered in a clear unhesitating voice, without consulting a note, were a startling denial of this.

He was driven to London by car every day long after he could have retired, and it was rumoured that he swam every morning before breakfast, winter and summer, in his unheated swimming pool in the garden. Certainly he swam every evening on his return from town. There were times when some of us had to make smart manoeuvres to avoid embarrassment. He always swam naked. Occasionally on a warm summer evening he would cross the lawns on his way back from a swim and sit on the terrace, still naked.

He had given permission to the nurses from the Forest Hospital next door and some of us with young families to use the pool each evening after school; just so long as we were out of the way before he wanted to swim. Usually all was well; but since he was a law unto himself, if he returned early from London on a hot day, he could complicate our plans. Once or twice we stumbled on a strange apparition, and beat a discreet and hasty retreat.

His daughter Enid, a Froebel-trained teacher, quiet and kind, ran the family home, St. Just's, with a minimum of fuss and still found time to be involved in a number of good works. The house was full of treasures collected on trips abroad. I had nightmares when, with other young mothers, I took small children to tea there. Enid thoughtfully provided toys, but there was a gilt grand piano in the drawing-room, much silver-gilt, and huge valuable Chinese jars standing on the floor. The children were active and not used to avoiding priceless treasures. I watched them with some apprehension. Yet, I think if there had been a calamity, Enid would have told us not to worry, and assured us that it was not important.

Leslie Linder, her bachelor brother, was also musical and had another grand piano in his room. He was reserved with adults, but interesting if he could be prevailed upon to talk; he was happiest with children, with whom he was perfectly at home. He was a brilliant mathematician and by profession an engineer expert in mast design and erection. He was also a generous benefactor to our church, providing a wonderful children's library, which he presided over every Sunday morning after service. Our children remember this library as one of the most important influences in their lives. Hundreds of books for children of all ages were on the shelves, ranging from the classics, through A.A. Milne, Alison Uttley, Beatrix Potter, Catherine Nesbitt, Arthur Ransome to every recognised children's author, all in attractive condition, and added to constantly. I am sure he experienced great satisfaction from this library and the contact it gave him with so many eager and delighted children.

They had only to ask for a book not on the shelves for it to appear the following week. He taught the older children to appreciate beautifully bound and illustrated books, and trained them to help him with the indexing and borrowing records; and he also found time to research and write his famous definitive work on Beatrix Potter. Only the fact that from time to time a tall mast appeared in the ground of St. Just's reminded us that he had other skills and a professional job. To us his gift of the children's library was unique and memorable.

Chapter XVIII

Friends

Some families attract people into their circle like moths to a lamp; sometimes by their vitality and sincerity, their generosity or sheer good will. The Mann family who came to our church from Chigwell — always late, sweeping down the aisle to seats in the front row during the first hymn — had just this gift of friendship. G and I were welcomed into their life and grew to know them well, enjoying the warmth, stimulus, and confidence they engendered.

Joyce Mann, the mother of a grown-up family, was a very special person. She was tall, broad-shouldered, quietly but never very smartly dressed, with a comfortable bosom and a sympathetic ear, adored by her family of two sons and three daughters with whom she shared a lively sense of humour and a deep understanding. She was a member of the Somervell family from Kendal who owned K shoes; her brother was Dr Howard Somervell, known as Uncle Hunch, who had been doctor on the first Everest expedition. She was rich and colourful, amusing, outrageous, open-hearted, and totally without cant and pretentiousness. Her religion was real; "the Lord" was a friend to her, part of her everyday life, with whom she could converse at any time; she was down to earth, with no pious moralising.

They were a distinguished family: Gerald Mann, her husband, was an Oxford classical scholar and managing director of the family firm of Howard's, of Howard's aspirin fame; their elder son, William Mann, was music critic to *The Times*; their eldest daughter, Pauline, was an artist married to Norman Del Mar, the conductor. Benjamin Britten was a close friend. People and music filled their house. Paintings and books, arguments and discussions were part of daily living. So too, was cooking for numbers of visitors, who were fed in the kitchen without fuss, but with good food and wine and conversation.

Marchings, their comfortable rambling house in Gravel Lane, Chigwell, dated from the eleventh century and had been one of King John's Hunting Lodges. Joyce was no slave to it and swore she never dusted more than once a week, and even then she was chided by the family not to become a "Woodford housewife". The gardens were charming and demanding: you were urged to shoulder a tool to attack weeds if you decided to explore its depths. An immaculate croquet lawn had pride of place.

Three of the younger children were still based at home; her son, Bobby, Susan and Helen, usually known as Pussy. They lived easily with her, sharing her sense of humour and adopting her familiarity with "the Lord". I remember

64: Joyce Mann

Susan at eighteen standing with her arm round her mother's shoulders assuring me with a grin that they had an Oedi-*puss*-ian relationship. Helen wrote home from boarding-school one day to say that she was in the "San" with some normal complaint, which I have forgotten, but which fortunately meant that she had missed some exams, for which as the Lord knew, she had not revised. He was evidently on her side.

I was flummoxed by the exclusive language the two girls sometimes practised and when Susan was once driving me and the children home, I demanded to know why she muttered, "Hengist, do get out of the way!"

65:   Joyce & Gerald Mann in London

66: Marchings, the Manns' eleventh century Hunting Lodge at Chigwell

67: Joyce striding off to attack weeds at Marchings, with Bobby & Gerald Mann, and David Somervell

apparently exasperated by the driver of the car in front who was irritatingly slow. "Why Hengist?"

"Oh Hengist and Horsa, you know," she airily replied, "Horsa – nausea – nauseating!"

A somewhat tenuous connection, I felt, but family languages, as in the Mitford family, are notoriously obscure to the outsider. The Manns had a similarly devious word connection when referring to their new combined bathroom and loo as the "United Kingdom".

Richard and Geoffrey Crossman, whose mother, Lady Crossman, lived at the top of Queen's Road, Buckhurst Hill, were their cousins, so it was no surprise to find that the Manns supported the parliamentary Labour Party.

One day as I was pushing the pram back from Nursery class, a large old Riley passed me then pulled up suddenly and Joyce bundled out and hurried after me.

"Nan, do you think I ought to join the local Labour Party?"

"No, I don't," I laughed back at her, non–plussed by the sudden question. I wondered what on earth the local party members would make of this upper–middle–class woman interjecting impulsive remarks with perfect sincerity but a marked Oxford accent. Apart from providing transport for Labour supporters on Election Day (Gerald shirtless and dressed–down in a sleeveless vest), their politics were the intellectual socialism of the *New Statesman*, and one of their many generous gestures was to give G and me a subscription to the *New Statesman* during their lifetime.

No-one in the community was ill or in need but Joyce was there to help in practical ways as well as to offer comfort and compassion. She had her own methods of helping the church on fête days. There she was, behind an amazing White Elephant stall, full of real treasures in china and glass bought by her over the months from sales and auctions at country houses for miles around, now selling them at ridiculously cheap prices. Dealers got wind of these bargains and arrived to take advantage of her prices. She was indignant; in the end they had to be refused admittance.

"These prices are only for church people," she protested.

I certainly was grateful to buy, among other things, a beautiful set of half-a-dozen large Spode soup plates for half-a-crown each.

She harboured a constantly surfacing guilt complex about being privileged. Both her sons had been educated at Winchester, and several times she said to me,

"Do you think it was quite wrong to have sent them there?" and we would endlessly discuss the question of privilege, class distinction and equal opportunity. When the system of Comprehensive education came in, one of her sons sent his children to the local Comprehensive school and was delighted with it. She felt better then. I did point out to her that since he lived in Wimbledon, the catchment area did not offer any serious dilemmas.

It was this constant questioning and reappraisal in one so blessed materially, with a close and loving family who shared her sense of the ridiculous, and a wealth of friends, that made her such an endearing person. It was a privilege to have shared her faith and laughter. Joyce Mann was an enduring influence on those of us of a younger generation, bringing up our families in the aftermath of the war.

Remarkable people have been signposts and an inspiration to G and me at every stage of our lives. There were so many radical changes taking place during and after the war which challenged our deeply engrained attitudes, and since we were not then exhaustively confronted with television pundits or documentaries on every issue, we tossed ideas about among ourselves and our friends.

A new young couple arrived, also attending our church. The Martins looked daunting at first. Denis was thin and thoughtful, over six feet tall, and Jean was tall with raven hair, wearing a smart broad–brimmed black hat. I plucked up the courage to ask her to make a cake for some function.

68:    Dr. Denis Martin at Westbury Lodge nursing my Nigerian god-son

"Thank God someone's asked me to do something. I thought no-one would ever ask."

She need not have worried. Ever since, she was inseparable from catering at most functions.

Denis Martin was a psychiatrist and physician-superintendent of Claybury Psychiatric Hospital, South Woodford, in the fifties and sixties. Claybury was an enormous Victorian building in spacious grounds with two thousand beds in huge dormitories, wide long corridors which seemed to require transport, or at least roller skates, to traverse them without exhaustion. Denis was one of the most gifted and respected psychiatrists of his time, remembered for his pioneering work on the treatment of mental patients, expounded in his book, *Adventure into Psychiatry*, published in 1962.

From the beginning of his career, he recognised that traditional methods in mental hospitals were failing: doctors were all-powerful, taking decisions without consultation, failing to treat patients as whole people, and too often unsuccessful in their treatment of fundamental disorders. For several years he worked on an experiment in setting up a therapeutic community within the hospital where doctors, staff and patients could meet in regular groups for open discussion and participation. It was a revolutionary idea, laying the doctors and staff open to criticism from patients, and many found this difficult to accept. It was the death knell of the traditional invincibility of the medical hierarchy. But with perseverance, it worked. An atmosphere of mutual trust between patient and staff was built up, violence and locked rooms virtually disappeared, and daily life in the hospital became more cheerful and relaxed as the success rate with patients rose dramatically.

Denis Martin's book propounds his theories and recounts the gradual change in relationships and the invaluable training psychiatric nurses were getting by taking part in the therapeutic group meetings which were the basis of his new approach. Today his methods are generally accepted. In fact his non-authoritarian concept of understanding through discussion is now more widely applied, as he had hoped, in church and school communities.

By training, Jean Martin was an occupational therapist, practical and uninhibited, and an enormous support to Denis in his experimental and dedicated work. She had no pompous ideas about psychology in the home and averred laughingly,

"We don't have any psychology in our house!"

I went with her to a series of ecumenical discussion groups at the vicar's. She would cut through somewhat highfaluting expositions of dogma with down-to-earth comments, and she dumbfounded the traditionalists one day by stating firmly,

69:    The Towers, attached to Claybury Hospital

"Well, I don't really need Christ anymore: I've found God."

They said nothing, but looked askance. I knew just what she meant. The ultimate end is to find truth, or God; Christ, as the image of God in man, was the means to the end. But we were regarded as heretics, and the argument drifted into silence.

Denis and Jean lived with their three daughters in a large house, The Towers, attached to the hospital, with no locked doors in between. Jean recounts with amusement the morning she came down the stairs only to pass a patient on the way up, saying earnestly,

"I must just speak to the doctor."

I should have found such an invasion of privacy intolerable. He lived as he taught — open to everyone.

It was significant that when a group of friends met at their house on Sunday evenings, with no set topic, but talking about anything under the sun, Denis was reluctant to be in the chair or even to initiate a subject. He much preferred to stand on the sidelines sharing and commenting on an equal basis. We accepted this, but there was no doubt of his intellectual stature among us, and we turned to him often to express his opinions and guide us to conclusions. He was a very modest and caring man, who taught us much, and gave to me a belief in holistic medicine; I have never forgotten his statement that "disease is dis–ease."

He deflated me too. When our youngest child started school I went back to teaching for five years and when I decided for domestic reasons that it was time to retire, I was heavily involved with the top class and their examinations. Perhaps we all have delusions of immortality. I rambled on about my commitment to these children, in effect, wondering how on earth they would manage without me. He laughed at me.

"Good Heavens! You won't be immortal, Nan. Do you really think God can't manage without you?"

I took his point. None of us is indispensable, however flattering it is to think so.

Chapter XIX

New Towns and a New Job

Mulberry Green is the attractive centre piece of old Harlow. Mother's flat was in an enviable position. On one side was Mr Young's shop, and on the other a large Georgian house, red-bricked and bay-windowed with a mellow brick wall, which throughout our life in Matching had been the home of two bachelor doctors, Tim and Newcomb Day. They were like chalk and cheese. Tim had been our family doctor, visiting us at Woodville rather than expecting us to attend his surgery in this house on Mulberry Green. He was tall with curly grey hair, dressed in a tweed deer-stalker hat and a heavily-caped cloak. He sat like Sherlock Holmes behind his uniformed chauffeur, making magnificent progress through the villages in all weathers in an open tourer. Newcomb, far less flamboyant, could have been mistaken for a business man in his trilby and dark-striped suit, modestly driving himself around his practice in a small snub-nosed Morris.

When the two doctors died, the house was empty, but within a few years it was sold to the Harlow Corporation to become the central offices of the new Harlow Town in the process of erection, spawning in neighbourhood areas to the south-east of the old town, engulfing the villages of Burnt Mill, Parndon and Nazing, all places to which my father had cycled every week to collect the names of absentees from the village schools, when he was School Attendance Officer.

The doctors' house gave Mulberry Green an air of distinction. The grass was not a stretch of course tufts, but a mown lawn stretching from the front of the house to the road and across on the other side, spread out in front of the houses and a row of small cottages at the top of the hill.

In one of these had lived Nurse Armour, a Harlow district nurse, who for some obscure reason, probably the illness of the Matching district nurse, had attended Mother for my birth in 1913 at Woodville, a three-mile cycle ride way with hardly a house to show any cheer from a lighted window at night. A visit to Mulberry Green when I was a child was also a visit to Nurse Armour. "Your nurse, dear," Mother would say, as if she were a private employee.

On the other side of Young's shop was Mr Clarke's blacksmith's forge, tucked up against The Green Man, then a wooden-framed country inn; now a smart much-advertised smart Trusthouse Forte Hotel, vying with the old Georgian house as the centre of attraction on the Green.

When she first lived in the flat, Mother could walk with difficulty from Mulberry Green to the High Street to shop; but as her feet and hands became

71: ... becomes the first administrative office of Harlow New Town

70: The batchelor doctors' house on Mulberry Green ...

more deformed by her crippling arthritis, she became housebound, and was only able to be taken out in a wheelchair.

Mother had a spell in St. Margaret's Hospital in Epping, and when she went back to the flat, Aunt Lizzie from Stoke-by-Nayland, her usual supportive self, came to stay for a while, quietly taking charge and nursing her back to reasonable health. But it was no permanent solution. We advertised for help with little response. Eventually she shared her flat with a young couple without a home on a tenuous business basis: they looked after Mother, and in return had rent free accommodation and a small emolument. It was not an unqualified success. They gave her some mobility and occasionally pushed her wheelchair quite a long way, past Churchgate Street and up the winding Moor Hall Hill to Housham Hall to visit Hilda Tinney. It can't have been easy for them to spend their time with an elderly stranger, and Mother, in spite of her disability, still held the reins; but although they were kind, they treated some of her treasures with scant respect. Visitors were a problem. It was an uneasy relationship, and as Mother became worse there was no alternative but to bring her to live with us at Buckhurst Hill.

The house we had thought plenty big enough for our growing family was becoming distinctly crowded. Of the three bedrooms, we had the front one, the girls shared another, and in between, Grandma Collecott had the spare room. Downstairs, John had the middle room as a bedroom, and our treasured front room had to house a divan for Mother. She could at least see out of the bay-window over the pond and Green to the Church and watch the passers-by. The breakfast-room-cum-kitchen became the family living-room. G and I promised ourselves to look round for something bigger, probably a property run down as a result of the war, which we could do up ourselves and make into a rambling old family home. We were ever optimistic.

In the meantime, in 1948, G had changed jobs. He still remained under the same authority, the Essex Education Committee, but he was appointed Warden of a Community Centre and Youth Group, which he was to set up in the new town of Hainault, then being built between Grange Hill and Chigwell Row, facing the ancient Hainault Forest. Hainault was to accommodate thousands of Londoners to be moved into Essex from the East End. It seemed like a trial project for the spate of new towns which sprang up as a result of the war, culminating in the largest and best-planned at Harlow under Sir Frank Gibberd's direction.

It was a challenge. G was ready for a change.

When we were children we had often heard of collections in our village churches, and notices in Parish magazines, for something known mysteriously as "London over the Border". It sounded as if it had Scottish connections, but we had vague ideas that it referred to people moving out from London, who had to be accommodated in Essex where there was insufficient money in our parishes and churches to "minister to them" adequately. This post-war migration was a very different matter.

When G was appointed, only part of the new town was built. I went with him to survey the area. There were rows and rows of terraced houses, with a modest attempt to use varied building materials and a variety of designs, colours and textures to break the monotony: but I was appalled. To me they looked box-like and cheap, lacking in inspiration.

G was more tolerant; born a Londoner, he knew how good was the position of these houses, with their immediate access to Hainault Forest, yet near the underground Central Line for residents to return easily to their work places each day. I was not convinced that a lack of imagination is always governed by a lack of money. Those houses were uniform and dull. It seemed a pity to miss an opportunity to create a pleasing environment, and it was not an adequate excuse that, after the devastation of their area in London, people would welcome new homes with modern amenities.

G was soon to find that the whole scheme had been started without sufficient forethought and planning. People were being moved out into houses without any parallel provision for churches, pubs or community halls. There was little attempt at landscaped neighbourhood areas to stimulate a community feeling. But at least Essex Education Committee was building new schools to cope with the children.

G was to set up a Youth Centre in one of these schools. He was told to order equipment and choose materials for curtains in the hall. This was a major pleasure for us both. We had a long wall of glass windows to cover. This was the new era of school building which provoked much criticism. With hindsight the planners were told that such vast expanses of glass were too cold in the winter, too hot in the summer, a distraction from work and very expensive to curtain. We felt they were a welcome change from so many remnants of Victorian schools with high windows and dreary surroundings. Essex was to be congratulated: they were employing Gerald Holton to design their curtain materials. G and I had visited his workroom in Tottenham Court Road when he had first set up shop and had been delighted with his work. In fact, we had bought one of his woven Cyprus carpets to cover our bedroom floor just before the war broke out.

Now we pored over swathes of original and colourful designs. A whole wall gave such scope for a bold and arresting design; at last we could put behind us the boring materials of the war period. We finally chose a heavy-duty blue linen, patterned all over with the backs of yellow and brick-coloured gypsy caravans, large splashes of colour, some caravans with a jaunty bucket hanging on the decorated back rail. They were gay and splendid. We were so enchanted with them that when G had finished measuring up the hall we added a separate order of our own in the same design. We would use them for the playroom when we found our bigger house. These curtains have been a joy for ever: I still have them.

For weeks G tramped the roads in Hainault, meeting people, discussing their interests, trying to assess their needs for leisure activities and possible evening classes, looking for suitable buildings, grumbling about the lack of amenities. The Youth Centre could start in a school building; the Community Centre needed its own premises in order to offer an effective meeting place. Slowly he got the project off the ground, finding people with skills to help, professionals to take evening classes and a variety of well-meaning people with a social conscience anxious to combat loneliness and disorientation for those families finding it difficult to settle down in completely different and often unsympathetic surroundings.

These eight years from 1948-1956 when G was at Hainault, were in many respects harder for me than the six war years. Our time-clocks were difficult to synchronise. When he was into routine, he spent the morning at home when I was too busy too notice him, and left after lunch. Without a car he was

72:    Diana helps out at a children's party at Hainault Community Centre

73: G and I at Hainault Community Centre. He is presented with a silver salver on leaving

dependent on an infrequent cross–country bus service, and he rarely caught the last bus home at night. This meant at least a good hour's walk home since we lived miles away. Unless the weather was wretched, he enjoyed the walk, however late; it gave him a chance to unwind, but he often arrived home at midnight, hungry for a substantial meal. I always sat up for him; after a day with two grandmothers and three children, I needed time alone with him.

A year later it became imperative to wait up for him. Mother had to be carried from divan to chair; usually G did this before he left at mid–day, and sometimes I could manage to lift her back into bed. More often, I had to wait for him to do it at night. It was distressing to see her in so much pain. She was such a frail skeleton that she found it impossible to lie comfortably for long on the softest of mattresses; every joint became sore and she couldn't shift herself to gain relief.

I marvel at how healthy we must both have been, for we never became depressed.

At times we were exasperated; Grandma Collecott was ungracious about putting coal on Mother's fire if I had to go out; Mother would assure me that she could eat nothing when I had cooked a full family meal, and then an hour later ask for scrambled eggs on toast. They were only irritating pin-pricks, and since we shared them, grumbled and laughed over them, they never built up

Chapter XIX

into a dispirited life-style. We were poor, but happy, with many friends and an energetic entertaining family whom we adored.

Occasionally, particularly for a special event, a friend would be a Granny-sitter, and I went to Hainault with G. Olde-Tyme dancing was very popular, and I loved to dance. Victor Madden, whom I have seen since in character parts on television, was a young actor then, gaining experience by teaching drama classes; he taught at G's Community Centre. I liked to see his productions. The people at the Centre were friendly and welcoming. I was impressed by their lively energy. They were made of sterner stuff than me, and were not dispirited with those uninspired rows of houses with a stark main street of shops. Sainsbury's to me seemed its only redeeming feature.

Back at Buckhurst Hill, on summer nights we put Mother to bed at midnight, ate a meal together, then strolled round and round the pond and Green, the darkness broken with street lamps along the High Road, ducks stirring in the water among the reeds, until the church clock reminded us that the next day had begun. Blessedly there were no more sirens.

G spent eight years as Community Warden in Hainault, watching the town and activities grow around him. Then we completely complicated life. In January 1950, Clare was five and starting school – and I became pregnant. John and Clare were a pair in looks and temperament, and have always remained close to each other. G and I agreed that to complete our family we needed a boy like Diana, and we never really had any doubts that it would be so.

But, what to do with Mother? Something would turn up we felt sure, though neither of us could have guessed how the situation would be solved. Mother thought I was dotty, but forbore to criticise, and in fact spent her time telling the doctor, when he came to see her, that he must look after me. He would come out of her room and say to me,

"You can't possibly cope, you know!"

I felt quite sanguine about it all. I'm one of those lucky women who feel at her best when pregnant: well and energetic, and thankfully without the rheumatic pains I had suffered when I was young.

74:    Housham Hall

75:    A later visit to Housham Hall, with Hilda Tinney on the right

Chapter XX

Camping the Easy Way

The baby would be born early in October, 1950, so we just had time to have a summer holiday first. The children longed to camp and G pointed out how simple life would be outdoors; no tidying up, a minimum of washing up, and there was no need to travel miles away. I was persuaded. I could imagine some slight discomforts, but there would be no need to keep up appearances; we could relax in the country and it would be easy and convenient to go back to Matching. I knew every meadow and neighbouring shed, and where there was a nearby supply of water and milk. It was no good worrying about shops and provisions; there were only two shops in the whole area, one on the Tye and one on the Green. I had no intention of doing the shopping, and both were in walking distance for G or John, who was going to be ten when his brother was born.

So Matching it would be. Hilda Tinney was now a widow at Housham Hall; we tried to see as much of her as we could, and she would enjoy having us on the farm. Mr Clarke, a builder who had done odd jobs for us and was the most kind and obliging person, agreed to transport us and all our equipment in his van. It took two journeys, because our number had increased to six as Diana had a bosom friend, José, who was joining us. We had already decided that four children were better than three when it came to games and pursuits.

First we had to organise the Grannies. G's brother agreed to keep an eye on his mother, and we prayed that she would be careful and not burn the house down in our absence. Mother we tried to book temporarily into a Nursing Home. At the beginning of the Fifties there was not yet a recognition that those caring for sick relatives needed short breaks, if only for a week while they went on holiday, so short-term care was much harder to find than it is today. We drew a complete blank. Then Pearl Newman's sister Claudia, a Sister-Tutor at University College Hospital, offered a possible solution. Lord Amulree, a consultant there, had a geriatric unit at St. Pancras Hospital, and he was a particularly sympathetic person. Dr Foster-Smith wrote to him and arranged an interview for us; so we took Mother to London by ambulance, an excruciatingly uncomfortable journey for her and for me.

G and I waited in the corridor. After examining Mother, Lord Amulree came out to us and said in his kind and encouraging manner,

"Don't worry. I will certainly take your mother into hospital by the end of August until after your baby is born. What's more, I'll see if we can make a real improvement in her condition."

We could hardly believe our ears, but we were moved and reassured by his word that all would be well.

Sometime before the end of August we had accumulated a formidable collection of objects which we were persuaded no self-respecting camper could be without. The children added a miscellaneous pile of games and books, and I contributed our most battered kitchen utensils and oldest clothing. If they were torn or caked with mud by the end of the holiday we could abandon them without a qualm.

On the last Saturday in August we set off, squashed into the van in stuffy proximity. We chose a small enclosed meadow at the end of Housham Hall drive, sheltered by the trees and hedges and well hidden behind sheds from the men on the farm going about their daily tasks. It was conveniently near to a water tap too. As we laboriously unpacked and the piles mounted around us, we noticed clouds gathering above and damp air settling down on us. We hurried to create order from the chaos, and were finally under cover inside our ineptly pitched tents when the rain came down. Undaunted we unearthed Wellington boots, sou'westers and macks and ventured out to explore the farm, visiting ducks on the pond, and the pigs squealing and tunnelling among the deep straw bedding in the yard.

The animals were all undercover and remarkably clean. We were in time to watch them being fed, with buckets of sloppy meal being poured into troughs, snouts buried in it and the pig-man poking the greedy ones out of the way to give the less aggressive a chance to fatten up too. It was going to be a short life before they were off to the market.

Then there was the ancient tithe barn to visit. It had stood there for generations; huge beams arched overhead, cobwebs festooned the corners, thick beams roughly hewn out of tree trunks were both vertical and horizontal, propping up the roof and defining its massive structure. There were bales of straw to climb on: the children were fearless, climbing almost to the roof on bales at ascending levels, avoiding the gaps in between them with amazing skill. There were piles of dry scented hay to tumble in, and dark corners to hide in; or a wide open space in the middle for chasing each other until they threw themselves cheerfully into the hay.

I had made old sheets and curtains into mattress covers, and we filled them with hay; as a concession to my advanced pregnancy I was allowed the only camp bed, an army officer's bed, unsold at the latest church jumble sale, and when it was erected, a great boon. It folded up into a miraculously small space and slipped into a waterproof case when not in use; but it required strong hands, skill and patience to put it together, since it had metal rods to slide into slots which always seemed too short and too narrow. No wonder officers needed batmen; otherwise their tempers each morning would have been intolerable.

It rained all that night and all the next day; trees dripped monotonously, views were blotted out. It was difficult to contain four energetic youngsters under canvas.

"Don't touch the roof, dear; the rain will come in!"

After breakfast on the next day, Hilda Tinney covered herself with a raincoat and hat from the hook behind her scullery door and plodded bravely across the soaking grass to us. She was worried.

"Are you really determined to stick it out?"

"It can't go on much longer," we protested.

""Well, why not move into the barn? It's not in use at the moment."

It was a splendid idea; hardly proper camping, but much more comfortable. We agreed with alacrity, the children only too pleased to help with packing up and removals. In no time at all we had made expansive hay beds on the floor, fitted up bales for a table and chairs, a washing–up bench, a shelf for utensils; there was no end to their usefulness. We tucked our belongings into corners, and the children helped us to divide the space into areas and were soon endlessly involved in games of schools, mothers and fathers, acting stories or just exhausting themselves with climbing.

G and John left the girls to play and went about the man's business of shopping. They had to walk over a mile to Matching Tye, either round the road, or when it was dry, across the fields and up the lane; They came back laden with provisions from the one and only village shop and Post Office.

On our first evening in the barn, Hilda popped a rice pudding in the Aga and brought it over to us for supper. It was the first of many. She shook her head over our seeming madness and hoped we kept from harm. Her real concern was for me, and she eyed me apprehensively.

"You won't have that baby here, will you?"

I was going to find it difficult to live down the saga of Diana's birth. I assured her that I had no intention of doing that; it was much too early to worry.

"Only a few weeks," she countered gloomily; then she cheered up and was her usual amused self. "You'll have to call it Barnabas, if it's born here."

We agreed, but prayed we should never have to saddle the poor child with such an outlandish name. Hilda told us later that she was so bothered about me that she finally rang up Dr Norman Booth in Harlow, my doctor before I was married, and told him how careless I was being and made him promise to be ready to come immediately if she rang him. He thought it was a huge joke and was not in the least alarmed; his reaction went some way to allaying her fears.

When the children were lined up, sound asleep in the hay, we sat in the barn watching the swifts swooping and diving over the pond, listening to the sparrows gathering noisily in the bushes as the evening shadows gradually darkened the sky. The rain had freshened the air. In turn, we slipped across to the house for a welcome hot bath. This was camping the easy way.

It turned into a splendid holiday. Alfie Whitbread was still foreman at Housham Hall and lived in a new cottage near the house. I remember it being built and we were full of praise for its modern Rayburn cooker. Edgar Tinney's reply had been typical.

"I'll have to put one in every cottage now. Might as well do it at once before they all ask for it anyway." He was well respected as one of the best farmers and employers for miles around.

Alfie, the foreman, had courted Gladys Crouchman from the Tye when I was a child. They had sat arm–in–arm in chapel on Sunday evenings and I had been at the church to take photographs of them still arm–in–arm on the wedding day. Now I was back, showing off my family and renewing ties with the area. It was strange to feel that a frightening and appallingly destructive war had gone on between these lives.

76: My photograph of Alfie and Gladys at Matching Church

Chapter XX

Superficially it seemed that time had stood still in the countryside; the lanes were still bordered with a variety of hedgerows, red and white campions and scabius lit up the verges and the almond scent of meadowsweet hung heavily on the air. I knew where the spindleberries grew, where to pick hazel nuts in the autumn, blackberries in the summer, and where ditches full of primroses were hidden from the road. But new barns were being built, farmhouses were smarter, and most of the Suffolk Punches which had lumbered down to the ponds in the evenings, muddying the water along the edge, were now replaced with tractors, lone machines cutting a brown furrow across a newly harvested cornfield. I missed the men gripping the plough handles and stumbling over the rough earth keeping up with a couple of horses pulling strongly to reach the end of a furrow, the men turning them skilfully with a tug on the reins, and on with the endless walking up and down. Farm labourers were slowly moving into a technological age; they were dry in the tractor cab, and many more of them would walk tall as they became old men, not bent and crippled with rheumatism and worn-out knee joints from hours on their feet over rough ground.

We were busily occupied for the whole fortnight in spite of the frequent showers. All our hopes of lying in the sun and looking as tanned as the gypsies in the couple of caravans parked on the verges near the Tye were fruitless. The sun was consistently coy. Actually it was difficult to distinguish dirt from tan on the children. Hot water was in short supply since it had to be heated on our old primus stove.

G had removed one side of a large deep biscuit tin, of a sort not seen these days when all biscuits are wrapped in neat rolls or packets, but which used to contain several pounds of loose biscuits and were lined up in rows in front of the grocery counter of the Home and Colonial or International Stores. G stood the primus in the tin so that it was protected from draughts, but made the pump accessible on the open side. As a child I had watched my parents use it regularly, but I feared and hated it and could not bring myself to use it. I was certain that it would flare up to unmanageable heights, or explode, and on this holiday, ignite the dry hay and straw. In my imagination the entire tarred barn was a raging inferno.

So, under G's management, we used it for cooking and washing up, and I occasionally gave the children a wash down, but usually it was a brief "lick and a promise" with cold water. By the last week their hair was dull and their clothes stiff with dust from the clouds they stamped out of the straw bales. Children and clothes needed a soak.

Fortunately it was time for school and school clothes when we returned to Buckhurst Hill. The children went in opposite directions: the girls to Loughton and John to Woodford with his faithful friend, Christopher.

The two boys had a passion for holes. They would arrive home late from school, having stood for an hour watching men digging a hole in the road. Then they attacked our depressing patch of lawn and dug an enormous hole in the middle of it, propping it up and covering it with a junk assortment of boards, poles and discarded mackintoshes. Finally they climbed into it, settle down on boxes beneath ground level, and asked me to bring their supper out to them there. It was one stage easier than handing it up to them on the platform of the tree house the family had laboriously built in the apple tree, so I obliged them. Two less indoors making a mess was to be encouraged. Was this a remnant of the war, and were they playing at air-raids, I wondered?

77: With Peter, born 1950, the family was complete

Quite unexpectedly, Mother died in hospital on October 6th 1950. She had been given penicillin to which she was allergic; I had forgotten to tell them this. A phone call informed us. I went into the Nursing Home the next day, and Peter was born early on the morning of October 8th. My grief was compounded with guilt.

"Don't cry, dear; you'll upset the baby." The nurses were kind and efficient.

The baby was a great comfort to us both; just what we wanted, healthy and lively, and physically exactly like Diana. We did as Mother would have wished and concentrated on the baby. As I had left for the Nursing Home, John had run after me to give me firm instructions,

"Don't bother to ring back if it isn't a boy!"

He was relieved and all of them delighted; the family was complete. We were not quite so unperturbed about the impending Nursing Home bill. We were finding it a struggle to make ends meet, and had a strict list of priorities each month as to which bills had to be paid. A birth was an irregularity, but had to take precedence. Our bank balance was non–existent, probably a minus quantity; the bank manager had never regarded us as satisfactory clients. Then came the solution. G had to collect Mother's effects from the hospital: there was her gold watch and wedding ring, her carriage clock she had taken for comfort, and enough cash in her purse to pay our bill. God was indeed "moving in a mysterious way".

Chapter XXI

Moving House

"I've found the very house for us. You may think it's too ugly!"

So G made his exciting announcement when he came back from Hainault one evening in 1951. I was eager to inspect it.

A large FOR SALE notice by a respected Loughton estate agent was attached to the fence. Inside this a twelve foot hedge almost hid the house from view and a luxurious bay tree near the front porch reached the attic windows. The house was on a corner site between Westbury Road and Westbury Lane, and it rejoiced in the superior name of Westbury Lodge. We should never live up to that. It had certainly seen better days and had once been surrounded by extensive gardens, which had been sold off in lots, so that the main gardens and tennis court sprouted modern semis along the third side of the square, and a large white bungalow on the other side. The house was left with a garden of only half an acre, but it was detached, with a stable now used as a garage; even with a lawn and flower beds, we could find room for a small vegetable plot.

To G's surprise, I did not reject the house as ugly. I was delighted with it. Certainly the shape was stolid, the Cambridge brick a dull yellowish–grey, and the roof of slate; but the windows were large and the main rooms lofty and spacious, a typical Victorian house with the grand and mean side–by–side, separating the owners from their domestic help. Double swing doors, one of them of baize, divided the small kitchens, badly equipped and with narrow tall windows, from the entrance hall and two large reception rooms with beautifully plastered ceilings and chased brass door–knobs leading out of a right–angled drawing–room. It should have led to charming gardens, but unfortunately a tall fence came up close to the windows so that there was only room for a path round that chopped–off side of the garden.

No matter; I had already reorganised the house completely in my mind, hung the curtains, and allocated bedrooms on my first visit. Two small servants' bedrooms with little black fireplaces were one each for the girls. Granny Collecott could have the erstwhile dressing room on the front, John the large guest room, Peter the charming boarded attic, and G and I would have the large bedroom in the centre of the house, facing north inevitably, but in a good controlling position. Bell pushes in all rooms rang in the kitchen, presenting endless possibilities for children's tricks; since I was the only one likely to answer the summons, they would be disconnected at the outset.

We went home and fetched the children to see what they felt about it. There was no doubt of their reactions. Six bedrooms, space and corners and

78:    With my daughter Clare

places to hide: they were enchanted. Home again, they put a large label, Westbury Lodge, on one of their money boxes and placed it in a conspicuous place on the mantel-piece. They would save their odd pennies so that we would be sure to buy it. We were very touched, though we had hoped that we had not made our permanently penniless state too obvious.

The estate agent was insulted; our offer for the house was ridiculous. He refused to consider it. Joyce Mann looked at us in amazement.

"But it's a splendid house. I know it well. Mrs Richardson lived their and had a beautiful home. Can you possibly afford it?"

We pointed out that maybe she hadn't been in it lately. It had housed several families during the war, and had been empty ever since, and would need a heavy mortgage and hundreds spent on it. She decided that we were even madder than she had thought.

We waited a year for it, keeping a regular check-up with the estate agent on the state of play. It remained empty; no-one wanted it except us. When we had almost given up hope, he came to us and offered it at our original price. He was glad to get it off his books. We celebrated our success with enthusiasm and the children danced with delight.

It was not so easy to get a mortgage, which was crucial. We owned our current house at 6 Hills Road through the remarkable kindness of its previous owner, a retired civil servant. When we were first married we rented it from him. A year or two later he visited us, evidently liked what he saw, and said,

"But it's a nonsense for you young people paying out rent like this, when you could be buying it. I'm happy to sell. Why don't we count the rent you have paid so far towards its price?"

G was the business head; he arranged a mortgage and we bought the house for a few hundred pounds. A man of property, indeed. It was a kindness which opened up for us all future possibilities of owning our own home. G had a philosophy which coloured all his dealings: you can rarely repay kindnesses, but you can always pass them on.

Whenever we have moved houses we have shamelessly relied on architect friends to vet them for us. Now, our friend Bob Foster, head of the firm of Tooley and Foster, who used to live across the Green, put on his oldest clothes and climbed all over the house, emerging much dirtier, and not very impressed.

"It's a totally ridiculous house. The only rooms facing the south and the sun are the kitchens, bathroom and cloakroom."

All we really wanted to know was if it was basically sound and not liable to collapse about our ears when the family pounded over it. He assured us that architecturally it was fine and had been well and substantially built. So we pressed on.

79:   Westbury Lodge, "a totally ridiculous house"

Chapter XXI

G tried several building societies but they were not impressed with our choice of property, and were inclined to think it should be demolished. Then one afternoon I answered the front door to a short portly middle-aged man in a grey raincoat and a grey trilby. He was a stranger, but announced himself,

"I'm the chairman of The Walthamstow Building Society. I've had an application from your husband, and I've just been looking at Westbury Lodge. You don't really want that house, do you?"

"But, of course, we do. It's just what we want." I replied with enthusiasm, preventing the baby from escaping outdoors.

"But it's going to need so much work on it. We could lend you the mortgage, but on certain conditions. At the outset it must be completely renovated and redecorated inside and out."

I couldn't think of anything better. Colours of paint and wallpaper flitted through my mind.

"It will be a major undertaking. We shall have to release the mortgage in stages. Are you really prepared for this?"

I assured him that it was our one aim, a project we should be devoted to, and persuaded him that he couldn't possibly refuse to lend it to us and that we were ideal clients who would love the property. He stood stolidly there, trying to sum up such an obviously crazy woman, finally shaking his head and saying with a grin,

"All right. You shall have it. Good luck. I'll be in touch with your husband."

We were on our way.

Mr Clarke, our builder friend, moved in with his men, and created chaos. As G passed by each day, he kept an eye on Westbury Lodge and reported progress. I chose paints and wallpapers for approval and frequented Ambrose's Loughton Sale Rooms for bargains. Our furniture was neither sufficient nor of the right scale for the rooms. I bid for two three-piece suites for £10 each and made loose covers. It was amazing how many friends had superfluous furniture and were only too happy to dump it on us. Altogether we acquired four more divans for a variety of reasons such as families shrinking or a move to a smaller house. For £5 we gained a beautiful mahogany dining table with extra leaves, which a friend had been bequeathed and had no room for. It doubled for table tennis, while our own dining table became a side table. Our solicitor begged us to take his mother's enormous oak sideboard, which he had tried to give to hotels and failed. The back had to be removed because the heavy glass was broken in transit, but it was quite beautiful, eight feet long with a polished grained top and two enormous cupboards with wonderfully carved doors of fruit and leaves. G used it for a desk ever after.

We finally moved in ten days before Christmas, with workmen still decorating and telephone engineers on the stairs. Three cheerful removal men installed us, stopped to drink quantities of tea, and as he left the foreman shook his head,

"Well I know my missus wouldn't move in anywhere just before Christmas!"

There was no crushing us. We looked round at the tea-chests with pleasure, and had a specially happy Christmas, with blazing fires from piles of off-cuts of wood to compensate for bare areas and a draughty hall. The dining-room hatch was still a gaping hole, but functioning. I had no help in the house and there was no way I was going to carry food through double doors and across the hall to the dining room. It was a simple operation to put a hatch through from the kitchen to one half of the drawing room, so the rooms were swapped, leaving the other half at right-angles to the drawing room as a playroom. The girls appreciated the novel hatch; they set up a café, invited their school friends, and served tea through it.

Généviève, Françoise's sister, came to stay. She sat by the fire and surveyed the room,

"Ce n'est pas élégante, mais c'est très sympathique!"

We were satisfied.

Chapter XXII

The Family is Complete

Before spring arrived the hedges had to be tackled. They were like the impenetrable forest keeping out Prince Charming. We were no Sleeping Princesses, but delighted to feel part of the outside world again, when G and John between them, with some difficulty, using a cheap imitation of a Black and Decker, took three feet off the top.

John was as practical as his father; he discovered a pile of unwanted bricks behind the conservatory, and was soon pursuing a favourite occupation, digging a hole in a corner of the garden, lining it with bricks and constructing a sandpit beside a small pool of water for Peter's use.

Our neighbours in the bungalow, parents of Jean Shillito, a great friend of ours, offered us a swing seat to adorn this paved area. They were both in their seventies and no longer had the strength to erect it, nor the desire to use it. This was a tremendous status symbol. However it was incredibly heavy, having no possible relationship to the lightweight, gaily upholstered garden seats of today. It had been made to their specifications by tentmakers when they were very young and loved to sleep outdoors on summer nights.

Once we had erected it without slipping a disc, we had to leave it up for the entire summer, and in fact the basic scaffolding remained up permanently.

It was made of thick grey tarpaulin with a neatly scalloped canopy, guaranteed to protect us from a torrential downpour, and held in place by poles as thick as young saplings. The frame was built of metal girders, supporting a six–feet long seat and back–rest of slatted wood, with sawdust stuffed cushions and hard bolsters, all of which could be converted into a double swing bed. G and I used it as a seat, but never as a bed. The children were much more venturesome. Often joined by school friends, they queued up to sleep our there. I had some idiotic idea that, even under these circumstances, the front door had to be locked at night, so one of those sleeping outdoors had the front door key tied on a piece of string round the neck. If they became frightened, or lonely, or were awakened by a thunderstorm, they could let themselves in and go to their bedrooms. I find it hard to credit that G and I happily went to sleep indoors while they were locked out. Life was gentler then; we had no cause to suspect that burglars or marauders were wandering around at night, and fear never entered the children's heads.

Mr and Mrs Davies, these friendly neighbours, were almost embarrassing in their desire to make us welcome. Whenever we gave a party, they insisted on lending us silver entrée dishes, causing a few quizzically raised

80:    A self-portrait of Mr Davies, our next-door neighbour at Westbury Lodge

eyebrows from friends who were well acquainted with the parlous state of our finances. Then on the morning of the party, Mr Davies in his smart city suit, white hair and monocle, would arrive with a box of fifty Players cigarettes. Strange to remember that in those days, we not only put numerous ash–trays round the house, but also small pots with a bunch of cigarettes in each. It was the custom; health warnings were unknown.

Bare spaces in the rooms were filling up fast. Joyce and Gerald Mann arrived from Chigwell very soon after we had moved in with a splendid cast–off: a radiogram and a cabinet full of 78 records. They had moved on to more sophisticated equipment and these were now surplus to their needs. We gratefully put them to use.

Year after year, as the children became teenagers, we cleared the largest room of furniture, piling it in the conservatory, rolled up the carpets, sealed then polished the floor with a polisher borrowed from Nancy Butler, put wooden chairs, borrowed from the church hall, round the walls, and gave a party to about thirty of their young friends. From among the records, "*Mountain Greenery*", Victor Sylvester's quick–step, became a tradition as the music for the first dance. Its jingle runs through my head now.

Shah, unfortunately, felt she was getting too old to walk down the hill to our new home, tackle such a big house, and trudge back uphill home again. She was right; it was far too much to ask of her, but we were reluctant to let her go. More than anything I missed her laconic comments and her sensational snippets from the *News of the World* on Monday mornings. She was missing out too; our first three children she knew well, but not Peter. He was the most equable of them all, busy and entertaining all day long, taken frequently off my hands by his older brother and sisters, who bossed, scolded and spoiled him — and taught him everything they knew.

Even as a baby, he had them all on toast. During the winter, no sooner had I sat him on the table and between us we had dressed him with difficulty in leggings, hat and gloves, ready to go out, than he would smile winningly at us and proceed to snatch off his hat and throw it with his shoes and gloves on the floor. Willing hands retrieved them, put them on again and the whole rigmarole would begin again, until I was exasperated and seized him, dumped him in a push-chair, and dared him to remove another thing.

Peter made no effort to talk when he was very young. It was totally unnecessary; the older children could interpret his every sound, shout or grunt, and fulfil his every whim. When it became necessary, he was perfectly able to converse in long sentences. John taught him to be skilful with bat and ball; the girls were set on educating him and read him stories, and taught him to read when he was four. He would sit entranced when G or I read to the older ones.

A friend drove us to Greenwich Observatory for Son et Lumière one evening. We sat on rugs eating our supper on the lawn overlooking the Old Observatory and Royal Naval College and I noticed that Diana was sitting close to Peter, and explaining the history to him.

G had made a puppet theatre for them out of a large box, I had sewn some curtains, and they had painted the scenes and invented the stories. They allowed Peter, under strict supervision, to take part in manipulating the puppets and cut-out figures on their stage. I was directed to provide refreshments in the interval, and G and I were the captive audience, usually willing, but paralysed with boredom when they were carried away with their drama and the performance grew longer and longer. Clare was artistic, but Diana had a high sense of drama. As one parent informed me, after the girls had spent a morning with her children,

"Diana has been dressed up all the morning, putting on a great tragedy queen act."

Settled at Westbury Lodge, we found our life fuller than ever. The children brought their friends home and visitors were frequent. Anne was established as a welcome Aunt, arriving with little warning and spending at least a week with us as she passed through London on her journeys abroad. Her subject was Geography and she was a compulsive traveller, arriving back with presents from all parts of the world: a teapot from Tashkent, a jug for spa water from Azerbaijan, a woman friend from Tehran who needed hospitality, and always books for the children. Then she would return a few months later with a projector and dozens of slides and give a masterly illustrated tour through the U.S.S.R., Mexico, the Grand Canyon, Persia or China. After a teaching exchange with Australia, she went back there, or to New Zealand, every year, and brought all her returning visitors to see us. Most people today are bored with each others' holiday slides; our family loved them, and may well have gained the interest they have in travel today. Back in Liverpool, Anne used them for lessons and lectures.

She was a loner, and since her Norwegian lover had returned to Norway and his wife and family after the war, she had always travelled alone, making friends as she went, or infuriating them with her bossiness, and was fortunately strong enough to hump her own luggage about. She recalled visiting one small town in the Australian outback, and asking an hotel employee, lounging outside the door, if he would carry her luggage to her room, only to get the drawled response,

"What's the matter with you? Are you a bloody cripple?"

I'm sure she had a suitable riposte.

By 1956 G had completed eight years at Hainault Community Centre and since the family was making greater demands on his time, it was more convenient to have a teaching post, so he moved to St. Barnabas' School at Woodford Green. With John now at Chigwell School, Diana at Loughton High School and Clare still at Oaklands, we had events at four schools to cover at the end of term and especially during Christmas festivities. I added to the confusion by taking a part-time teaching job when Peter was starting at a Nursery class.

It was all due to new raincoats. All schoolchildren, boys and girls, in the fifties wore uniform raincoats. John was growing leggy and his was too short. It was passed down to the girls regardless of buttons and button-holes being on the "wrong" sides; but he must have a new one. Taunton House, a small private school in Queen's Road, needed a qualified teacher; it was conveniently near, and although I knew nothing about teaching Juniors, I felt my own family had pointed me in the right direction. I would work for three mornings a week for a term. The raincoat was the target.

I was blacklegging by accepting a lower salary than that set by the Burnham Scale, but I enjoyed the job and it was convenient. I earned every penny. Numbers of pupils were dropping, fees were going up, staff was being pruned and the Headmistress had dismissed the catering staff and was teaching herself *and* cooking lunch. I was teaching the top class who were a bright scholarship group, and while she peeled the potatoes and prepared the puddings, I took two classes together in a crocodile across the road to a church hall where there was a piano, and we could country dance, sing or do "Music and Movement". I would extemporise wildly while they interpreted the music, creating storms, striding like giants, or huddling into a forest of trees. It was all very creative and exhausting, thoroughly enjoyed by small children, but scorned by the boys in a mixed class of older children.

The Headmistress took over in the afternoons, dosing herself with pills to keep going, and somehow finding time to breed a fascinating collection of budgerigars in cages in the hall. I picked up Peter from his nursery class and climbed the hill home to lunch before tackling the household chores.

At the end of the term the girls reminded me that *they* now needed new raincoats, so I carried on for a while longer. In fact I continued until Peter was five and ready to start at Woodford Green Preparatory School, where John had been until he passed his entrance to Chigwell School.

I took Peter to interview Miss Read, the Headmistress. She was cheerful, plump, and welcoming. When I knew her better, I found her a strict disciplinarian, but with a great love and understanding of children, particularly bright, energetic, boys. It was undoubtedly the school for him: busy, highly

81:    Peter, aged five, in his first school uniform

competitive, and full of activities and interests to challenge his energy and intelligence. Miss Read tested and accepted him, then turned to me and said,

"I want someone to take the top class. Why don't you come and do a full-time job? Peter's times and holidays will fit in with you."

She was persuasive; I was tempted, but I had to take the decision with all the family. It was bound to make a difference to each one of them. To my surprise John was the only one to disagree; and he was horrified.

"Mother, the boys can be awful. You'll never manage them. They'll play up. Don't go!"

He was evidently concerned to protect me from the cruel hands of fiendish eleven-year olds, and afraid too that I might let him down by succumbing to their machinations. I laughed at his fears; but they were not allayed until I had finished my first term there and had enjoyed it and emerged unscathed. I stayed for five years, until Peter reached the top class and moved on to Chigwell.

Chapter XXIII

A Remarkable School

Nora Read, Headmistress of the Woodford Green Preparatory School, is one of a small group of people who, whatever their circumstances, attract willing helpers. In her case there was a particular handyman, who solved her practical problems, put in more time than he was paid for, and happily responded to a variety of requests totally unconnected with the contracted job. At the school Mr Smith filled this role. Later in Miss Read's retirement, Mrs Fennell, her Home Help, and Mr Parker, her gardener, attended her with the same cheerful devotion, exercising her dogs early in the morning, doing her shopping, discussing her paintings and photography, and mending her tools. They never appeared grudging, and seemed perfectly content to be beamed upon, thanked and appreciated. It's a marvellous gift, and perhaps has something to do with charisma. Perhaps it also had something to do with her enthusiasm for life, whether it was gardening, about which she was very knowledgeable, or whisking a class of children to Dorset for a week to share her interest in geology.

The teaching staff were strangely attracted into the same aura. We worked long hours, often staying after school until five o'clock to help a child with a problem, cheerfully giving up a day of the holidays to return for a staff meeting, or attending one in the lunch hour. We rarely had a teaching period off, so struggled home laden with books to mark in the evenings. But there was hardly a grumble; we were a very happy school, and although she could be formidable, we had a great affection for her.

The children treated Miss Read with a healthy respect. After a Froebel training she had started the school from small beginnings, on firm Christian principles. It was now a thriving preparatory school, attracting children from professional homes from a wide area; its examination results and the future careers of its pupils were most impressive.

Every morning Miss Read took a masterly assembly of the entire school. At the beginning of the school year she stared with the Creation, and for half-an-hour each morning she told the children a story, slowly progressing through the prophets, kings and histories of the Old Testament until she moved on to the Gospels and St Paul's missionary journeys and letters, timing it all beautifully so that the end of the stories coincided with the end of the third term. I was particularly enthralled with her Old Testament stories. She had done her research and filled in the background, captivating their attention with her exciting narrative. After these thrilling stories, any church sermons must have been bitterly disappointing to them.

82: Norah Read, Headmistress of Woodford Green Preparatory School, with members of staff, 1949

84:	Sonia & Norman Potter, the first married couple among WGPS pupils, return to present prizes at Junior Sports Day, 1955; Norah Read on the right

83:	WGPS Footballers, 1950

A Remarkable School   147

She adored dogs, and had a faithful Alsatian in her study with her. I was scared of it, but there was never any shortage of boys offering to walk in front of me when I had to go and see her. They loved to exercise it, too. In retirement in Somerset she has always had a succession of Alsatians and Red Setters; six of them at one time. I threatened never to go and see her if they were loose in the yard; they were clumsy and tempestuous, even if they were not going to bite me. They had not been particular about that on one occasion when the butcher's boy called. Money had to change hands to keep it quiet. I protested to her,

"I'm sure they'll bite me."

She airily replied, "Over my dead body, dear!"

I was not convinced that one dead body more or less made any difference to them.

At school she was full of interesting projects and visits. I was soon involved in producing plays and taking groups to Hampton Court, to London to the Science Museum, or the Natural History Museum. A colleague and I regularly boarded the Underground with sixty pupils and travelled to South Kensington. Fortunately they wore scarlet blazers, so it was difficult to lose them.

These visits were no wild escape from work. In the morning Professor Alfred Leutcher of the Natural History Museum gave the group a lively hour's lecture wandering around among the fossils and the dinosaurs, and after eating a packed lunch in pretty sordid conditions, all of them had to produce sixteen drawings to illustrate the lecture. This was Miss Read's firm instruction. It produced great sighs from the children and I felt it was rather a tough assignment. I found myself perching on the stand of the huge dinosaur skeleton, pencil in hand, dashing off a stream of passable sketches of dinosaurs' eggs, or dagger-shaped thumbs, to a queue of red-blazered children so that they could have time to wander at will and search out the blue whale, which was really outside their brief for the day.

These visits were all part of the famous "How Things Began" series, which the BBC broadcast on radio for schools in conjunction with the Museum. Miss Read embraced it with enthusiasm. I had groaned with other parents when, ten years earlier, John had returned once a week from school with homework requiring him to write a page on the broadcast, and illustrate it with a drawing or painting covering another page. He had never asked for help with the writing, but began yawning when he still had the drawing to do. I was at hand to help. Our joint efforts worked well until I made the mistake of painting a lurid forest scene depicting the Carboniferous period when he had progressed to the Jurassic period. He never trusted my artistic efforts again.

85:    Ready for a school outing. Me between Eileen Hooper and Deborah Hedin

86:    Part of a class at Hampton Court

When it was Peter's turn I left him to his own devices except to draw a caveman where it seemed impossible to go wrong. Miss Read was still supervising this part of the curriculum, but either the series had altered over the years, or was combined with another one covering the facts of life. To my amazement I arrived one morning to find her at the top of the stairs leading to her study and my first-floor class-room, button-holing a crestfallen boy. Her clear emphatic voice reached me,

"No, James, this homework is wrong! The *semen* has to be put in the female's body to fertilise the egg ...."

I could not believe my ears; correct facts had completely outweighed any other considerations. Any minute she was going to be bogged down in difficult explanations; luckily James was too crushed to ask pertinent questions. My arrival put a stop to any further inquest on his incorrect homework. The subject was immaterial; he had to have the correct terminology. I thought it was hilarious, and retold it dramatically to an incredulous staff.

The two top classes were bored at the beginning of the summer term. Their fates for the following September were settled: the "eleven plus" was over, and Public School Entrance examinations were behind them. Somehow my colleague Eileen Hooper and I had to dispel this apathy, and stimulate them into activity without any obvious attempt to educate them.

A film was the answer. Everyone must have a part; no learning by heart and only rehearsals on location. It would be relaxing and fun, offer scope for invention, and be much less demanding than constant rehearsals for a stage play at the end of term.

All my life I've been regarded warily by colleagues as I have a habit of coming up with way-out ideas, and sweeping them along into unknown events on the crest of my enthusiasm. This was no exception. Miss Read gave the plan her blessing. Most of the staff welcomed the idea because the school would be the quieter without us all, and there would be two spare class rooms to use. Eileen Hooper thought the whole idea mad but interesting and so long as I devised the plot and kept the mob under control, she offered to bring her ciné-camera and do the shooting.

We were complete novices. I was ignorant of correct techniques for film-making. However, undeterred, I offered to arrange a story into possible sequences, choose cast and locations, and direct on the spot.

Since we lived on the edge of Epping Forest, Robin Hood seemed a suitable choice. The children were rearing to go the moment I explained it to them. One very fat, rather shy, good-natured boy, reluctantly agreed to be Friar Tuck, but brightened at the prospect of being allowed to fall into the lake in the Forest so that he could demonstrate his prowess at swimming. Immediately all those who could swim begged to be allowed to go into the water. Sequences were obligingly adapted; fortunately no one was drowned or caught pneumonia.

Then those who could ride fancied themselves galloping wildly across the screen. This was a tall order. I had no experience with horses; but one girl's mother kept a riding school and to my amazement agreed to bring five horses to the plains one morning. Maid Marion's ride with her escort and the ignominious exit of the Sheriff of Nottingham sitting backwards on a horse with Robin Hood's men in attendance was most impressive. Fortunately the riding instructress stayed to supervise.

Parents all entered into the spirit of the thing. They encouraged us by making their children's costumes — very simple and raw-edged for the men; rather gorgeous with steeple head-dresses for the Court Ladies — and even fortified us by arriving with flasks of coffee to cheer us on when we were camped on the plains for a morning with Merry Men practising with bows and arrows in all directions.

Fortunately our first ventures were with silent films. When we showed them on completion no parent heard me yelling instructions above the excitement. A local vicar lent his church as Nottingham Cathedral, a Forest Keeper allowed us to drive the Sheriff's men into the lake, climb trees, plan ambushes and fight in the glades. He sometimes came and watched with an enigmatic smile on his face, ruminating on what education was coming to. The children dressed and undressed behind trees, and apart from one boy who waded into the water with his school clothes instead of his bathing trunks, under his soldier's uniform, everything went well. After editing with the help of a kind friend, the film ran for thirty minutes, amused the children and their parents inordinately on Open Day, and only cost £10.

It was so successful that the following year we embarked on another more ambitious film of Tom and Huck, adapted from *Tom Sawyer* and *Huckleberry Finn*. The choice of story was obviously dictated by the type of children in the two classes. That year the boys were bright and original, but scruffy-looking. The only two characters to need serious make-up were Huck's father, Pap, and Jim, the escaped slave. Luckily our younger son, Peter, large for his age, was in the group and an obvious Jim. I could hardly expect any other parent to put up with dense black make-up all over clean shirts day after day. Even a bath failed to move it all: he was dirty for weeks.

Once more water was a major attraction. So we used Connaught Waters Waters in Epping Forest as the Mississippi River, hired a boat several times and had the usual scenes of falling in. Only good swimmers were allowed to do this, but when the film was shown, even I held my breath when I saw the boat tipping dangerously over as willing hands on board rescued "The Duke" from the water. While it was being filmed I was far too occupied yelling unnecessary advice from the bank to worry.

People in cottages near the school allowed us to walk through doors and their front rooms, or steal sheets from their clothes line, and each day when the sun shone they cheered us on as we set out to film near "the river" or on the plain. This entailed long treks on foot for me with most of the children, clutching odd properties and bundles of clothes. Each day my colleague took as many as possible in her car with the boot filled with more clothes and, after a week or two, distinctly battered props. She drove happily down lanes and over meadows, while we covered miles on foot and by bus.

So emboldened were we by success that the following year we rashly decided to tape speech to go with the film. Claire Meixner, a friend and fellow teacher, was my colleague this time. She coped with all the filming and suggested many original shots. We were encouraged and advised by her husband Mike, who nobly lent his ciné camera and helped us to edit the film. This time it was to be *Worzel Gummidge*. The scarecrow chose himself: a slow, untidy boy, strangely uncoordinated, but with a sense of humour and a creative bent. He could manage some peculiar dialect, I thought, but only realised when it was too late, that his speech was too slow to keep up with the picture. Another smaller boy insisted on being his wife, Earthy Mangold, on a small fairy cycle.

The story tells of two children, a girl and a boy, making friends with the scarecrows. Louise Jameson, now well-known as a television actress, played the girl, while mother, full of ideas and enthusiasm, helped with make-up.

A local farmer kindly let us traipse over his fields, one parent lent us her house and garden, and Jack Watling the actor lent Alderton Hall, his house in Loughton, as Scatterbrook Farm. The *pièce de résistance* was the final scene which caused me great difficulties because we needed a train and a station and the nearest ones were all on the Central Line and obviously unsuitable. We had to go some distance to find a steam train at a main line country station. Then one shot had to show the train drawing out, and another the train racing past with the two children waving out of the window. It was all highly organised and too ambitious, but fortunately, the end of the movie.

We heaved a sigh of relief; but then came the editing and taping the conversation to fit. My colleague and I squeezed all the actors into her front room with a central microphone hanging down and the film showing on a screen in the corner. I had written all the scripts for this film and we had used them throughout in order to fit the time, but it was hair-raising not to be able to speak, but only to gesticulate, when one of the cast was so enthralled at seeing himself chased by a herd of cows that he forgot to read his part. We had a very limited budget so we couldn't keep discarding efforts. Even now the tape lags behind the action: perhaps it has stretched, or perhaps we were just hopelessly amateur. In any case it has provided endless amusement, illustrated surprising powers of invention in children, and caused a great deal of fun. For that generation of pupils, the point of reaching the top classes was to take part in a film. Passing examinations was quite incidental.

Chapter XXIV

Into the Sixties

A policeman stood nervously on the doorstep. It was a warm sunny afternoon in the summer holidays. I greeted him cheerfully, but had no smiling response. He was a serious young man.

"I'm afraid there's been a bad accident."

My mind raced swiftly through the whereabouts of each member of the family, and a feeling of enormous relief, followed by guilt at such a reaction, flooded through me when he continued,

"An elderly woman, your mother-in-law, I think, has been knocked down on the High Road by a motor-bike. She's seriously ill at St. Margaret's Hospital in Epping. I'm sorry."

He came indoors and gave me details. She had stepped off the kerb to cross the road into the path of a motorcycle ridden by a young seventeen-year old boy. She was very deaf and would not have heard it; her vision was hindered by a row of trees along the edge of the pavement. She had multiple injuries and was still unconscious. The prognosis was bad.

G went to the hospital, and on his return the same evening, we had more visitors: the youth on the motorcycle and his father. They were nervous and shocked by the possible outcome of the accident. They came to express their concern, and obviously to see if we were thinking of prosecuting. The youth was not a tearaway, and since there seemed no hope of her recovery, would have to live with this tragedy for the rest of his life. G and I had no difference of opinion; in the circumstances, we could not possibly prosecute. They both thanked us and went home greatly comforted.

We had long sessions with the police, but we told them that with her deafness she would not have heard the vehicle approaching and we could not attach blame to the youth. She never regained consciousness and at the inquest the youth was exonerated.

I was the one to feel guilty for experiencing relief at the outcome. I could not imagine how I would have coped with a family of six and a physically damaged grandparent. The Almighty was once again "moving in mysterious ways".

We took the family off to Devon for a seaside holiday, hoping the distressing experience would be absorbed with the usual resilience of the young. Françoise's younger sister, Claude, came too, and to our disappointment, spent most of the long train journey reading a book instead of looking at the changing scenery which she might never see again. We were amazed when years later she brought her children to see us and talked of that same journey and holiday and remembered far more than we thought possible.

We had found the holiday address in the *New Statesman*; a cottage, inland from Beesands near Kingsbridge on the South Devon coast, owned by a young couple. I think G and I expected earnest socialists, probably part of what we called the "raffia and sandals brigade", but we were pleasantly surprised. They were ardent vegetarians, compulsive gardeners and home-cookers, but made us very welcome, fed us — "there are eight different vegetables in that stew" — and left us to our own devices. We were probably a disappointment to them: not sufficiently political, too conventional and engrossed with our family to spend time with them discussing weighty matters and putting the world to rights.

It was a long walk to the beach, down a rough lane, then through a thinly treed spinney sifting the sunlight which dappled us with shade, and across an undulating field, sloping down to the beach. The weather was kind. The days passed too quickly: the children swam, marked out hop-scotch on the sand, threw quoits or played cricket. We climbed on the rocks to sunbathe and ate our packed lunches there, away from the gritty sand. Sometimes we walked along the cliffs to the remains of the ghost village of Hallsands, where the cliffs had eroded and most of the houses had disappeared under the waves, only one desolate house remaining where an old woman refused to be moved until further destruction was imminent. Peter was only five, but managed to keep up with the rest of us, still striding along as we climbed the field back to the cottage in the evening, tired, and laden with all the paraphernalia we seemed to need to spend a day on the beach.

It was about this time, as the Sixties were approaching, that we tackled the question of television. We were stuck with radio, which had provided excellent programmes for children throughout their early years. Most of our friends had progressed to television, and thought we were still in the steam age, or suffering from inverted snobbery. Actually we could neither afford it, nor had we the leisure to enjoy it. The three eldest were facing O or A Levels and were adopting student attitudes and working in their own rooms. We met as a family for meals and we were not prepared to sacrifice conversation to a background of television.

We made a concession. Each holiday, beginning with Christmas, we hired a television, and consequently sat engrossed each evening, unable to tear ourselves away from it. It was a distraction so powerful that we postponed

87:   Riveted to our first television – in the holidays!

having one permanently until exams were over. Then we settled down to enjoy our black and white rented set for the next fifteen years.

Certainly we had missed some valuable programmes, but maybe we had put off for a few years a trivialising of things we valued, and a certain brand of cheap joke, which was soon taken for granted. I was aware of its impact on children at school. The less able latched on to stupidities, like substituting "duck pond" for "swan lake" and finding it very funny because they had heard it from comedians on television. One boy suggested that it was unnecessary to read books as it was much more interesting to watch television.

Television had not yet been introduced into schools. I could foresee that it was not going to be easy to use this marvellous medium, with its ability to bring places and history to life, to offer dramatisation of books in authentic settings, to illustrate problems with professional graphics, to introduce poets and artists presenting their own work, to see news and fabulous nature programmes in the making; and at the same time to protect their innocence from cheap humour, crass advertisements, violence and sexual innuendo.

The Sixties, we recognised, were going to be challenging; we could not have anticipated how difficult they would be. Teenagers were a new classification, unheard of in our generation. We were either children respecting authority, or we were out in the world as young adults looking for security in work; our time as students was more like an extension of school, especially for women. Now we had three teenagers. Much as we had enjoyed running a comfortable hotel for them and their friends, the pace was beginning to tell. I am never convinced that an Englishman's home is his castle: not when it houses teenagers. There's no way of pulling up the drawbridge; the morning will reveal young strangers in the spare bedrooms or sleeping on the floor, no milk in the fridge and an empty Nescafé jar.

So far we had been king-pins in their lives. Now, just when we thought we could get by, we found we didn't know the right clothes to wear for specific occasions — "Oh, Mother, *not* that hat!" — nor the right table-cloth to use when they invited friends to tea; not even the ability to sum up their friends. If I proffered a mild opinion, which I thought would be pleasing — "James was nice!" — it brought the response, "Oh Mother, he's feeble"; or to "Sue was great fun!" back came the reply, "Oh no! She never stops talking." There was no way we could win.

We were challenged from all sides from the trivial to the fundamental. Stresses even developed between G and me, when we disagreed in our responses to them: I tended to condone; G was more authoritarian. Having played a positive role as parents for so many years, it was not easy to adopt another relationship immediately.

The girls dressed in all black like the rest of their peers; we tried not to remonstrate. It was no longer necessary to dance in couples since everyone appeared to be doing his or her own antics, and the music seemed unnecessarily loud so that we wondered if the decibel level would damage their hearing. Sometimes we sat up half the night with them discussing everything under the sun from religion, pornography, drugs, premarital sex to the atom bomb. Over the years we had tested and rejected many of our beliefs; but the certainties which remained we were determined to defend. We were not going to opt out, and they needed us as stick-in-the-muds and not trendy parents, so that they might feel more secure in a rapidly changing world. They might reject our guide-lines, but by providing some kind of yard-stick, we hoped they would realise that we cared deeply.

G and I emerged like chewed string, sometimes feeling depressed and outraged, especially if I was told my argument was phoney, and G was dismissed as pompous.

Diana went off on the Aldermarston March at Easter, and I toyed with going too, but had not the courage. I provided her with sandwiches, and hoped that she would not be put in prison and damage her chances of a University place. We listened to the virtues of Transcendental Meditation and recognised its value in relaxation, but thought sitting in a Yoga position while meditating

88: G survives the 1950s and 1960s

was unnatural, and were filled with misgivings about the role of the Maharishi. It was all too dangerous for our conventional, non-conformist inclinations.

We found Clare at sixteen reading *Lady Chatterley's Lover*, and wished she hadn't because it might have been very disturbing. I suggested offhandedly that Lawrence was rather turgid, but got very little response, so made no effort to pursue it.

At their age we were introduced to little more revolutionary than detergents and sliced bread; they had to cope with the terrible implications of

89: The author survives too: 1960

Chapter XXIV

splitting the atom, the very real fear of nuclear war, and the Pill which revolutionised life for women and changed the established relationship between the sexes. Women's fight for their rights and equality put marriage in jeopardy, and they experienced a more difficult choice between a career and marriage. As parents we felt challenged too. Alvin Tofler assured us in *Future Shock* that to survive we must adapt. G and I discussed it endlessly, and made an effort to adapt, without throwing overboard our deepest convictions. To accept that marriage was not a lasting commitment was impossible for us personally, but we learned to adapt sufficiently to appreciate that it was not always the best solution to prolong it in all circumstances.

Fortunately our friends were all floundering along at the same time and we could compare notes. We could also share our lighter moments. When John had taken a new girl friend out for the evening, he would sometimes arrive home long after midnight, but would wake us up full of excitement, sit on the end of our bed, and regale us with an account of his marvellous evening. We were delighted to be treated to such confidences, but stifling yawns and endeavouring not to sink back to sleep was quite a problem. They were exhausting times, but keeping open house and meeting lively and stimulating young people kept us, if not abreast of the times, at least striving to understand them. Fortunately we were far too busy to be self-indulgent in agonising about the challenges of the Sixties. So far we had taken life in our stride and had sufficient confidence to know that we would weather any storm.

After the war and its dreary aftermath, the Sixties challenged us all with its protests, its vigour and its new attitudes to life. For G and me it brought a considerable battering, but also a feeling of being part of a new upsurge of spirit and a new width and expansion of living in many fields; and not least amongst its compensations, the acquisition of the sturdy old second-hand Ford.

G conquered it first, then two of the three older children, and then me. All of them passed the test the first time – except me. Backing was a problem; I excused myself with the reminder that I was very short, and it was quite difficult to see out of the back windows. It was no easy car to drive, since it was necessary to double-clutch to come down into first gear, the hooter button was awkwardly placed in the centre of the steering-wheel, and all signals had to be by hand. This meant risking pneumonia by driving in winter with the window down so that one could thrust an arm out to turn right, and gently rotate it to turn left. I, of course, kept the window down all the time for ease, until the family swore they were perishing with cold and refused to ride with me.

When I passed my test at the second attempt, the examiner remarked casually,

"Well, if you can drive that, you can drive a bus."

That was all very well for him with his nippy little Triumph Herald, which could turn round on a sixpence. We were more sedate.

Before the Sixties were through, all the family had left home: to study, to follow a career, or to marry. G and I were on our own again; and mobile. Cycles had restricted our range. Now we could explore further afield, discovering first more of the byways of East Anglia, the lone landscapes and clear skyscapes of the Norfolk coastline, then on to the Yorkshire Dales, the grandeur of Northumberland and the charm of the Welsh valleys.

Nearer home we could now drive to Matching in an hour to visit friends: before this it used to take us an hour by coach followed by an hour's walk from Harlow. Matching airfield was outside the perimeter of the village, and by the time we visited it, almost all the buildings, except the remains of the Control Tower and a useful hangar, had disappeared. The land had reverted to farming. Just a faint whiff of nostalgia remained for me. Harold Parsons from Stock Hall, and later from New Upper Hall, used a hangar for storage. Among his stores, and still in use, was the chassis of his Sunbeam Talbot, now relegated to a useful but undignified life, moving sacks and machines. In its heyday in the early Thirties, a gleaming black Tourer, it had been the object of great admiration. I remembered it with all the excitement of an eighteen year old, just about to leave for college, when Harold drove us along the old A11 to Cambridge, touching the dazzlingly impossible speed of seventy m.p.h.

Now the Americans had returned home from all the Essex airfields, which had nearly all disappeared under the plough. It was another world.

— The End —

Index